GETTING THERE

Cynthia Carbone Ward

Printed in the United States of America

For all the travelers who sometimes feel lost.

Cover art by Kam Jacoby
Layout and design by David Richards

ISBN 978-1493641000

Sacate Canyon Press
Gaviota, California

I STEPPED from plank to plank
So slow and cautiously;
The stars about my head I felt,
About my feet the sea.

I knew not but the next
Would be my final inch,—
This gave me that precarious gait
Some call experience.

Emily Dickinson

Foreword

Think of this book as notes from a journey, written in the hopes of sharing lessons I have gathered along the way, discovering the meaning I may have missed, and sometimes asking questions still unanswered. A few of its essays are set in the pre-hipster Brooklyn of my childhood, an old-fashioned, working class neighborhood where the kids of immigrants played sidewalk games. In the early 1960s, my family became part of the great exodus from the city to Long Island, a place still in its adolescence then, as was I, and some of the stories are from those Long Island days. Many meanderings, detours, false starts and downright stalls were to follow, but my trip finally appears to have culminated here in California, a fact that seems somehow both unlikely and inevitable. It's not just any California, either, but a cattle ranch on the central coast, a little like the 19th century but with Internet access, a point of no return near Point Conception.

The stories herein are not always arranged in linear or chronological order, so be prepared to feel unmoored occasionally, as indeed we do in life. Many details and names have been changed, and I've allowed myself the liberty of a little invention here and there—but every piece is essentially honest. No doubt others saw things differently, but these are my tales and my truths.

I am grateful to dear friends who read these pieces, encouraged me in my writing, and helped me with this book, most especially Dorothy Jardin, as well as Christine Beebe, Cele Donath, Daniel Gerber, Vickie Gill, Kam Jacoby, and the faithful members of the Gaviota Writing Group started by the late and beloved Bob Isaacson. (Here's to Bob—he was the best of us, the heart of us, our story catcher and poet.)

And thank you to Monte, for his unwavering patience, love, and support.

Finally, the memories of my father, my brother Edward, and my sister Marlene imbue anything worthy I have written and everything hopeful I do. They are forever in my heart.

Contents

Leaving

When I was about thirty years old, I saw that my life had gotten away from me and I had to make it my own. Weary of New York winters and with little to lose, I decided to go west, defying the chorus of caution and disapproval that I see in retrospect must precede everything big we ever do. I crammed my possessions into plastic trash bags and drove away in a '73 Buick, avocado green, with a vinyl roof whose tattered strips blew like sails in the wind, seats strewn with trash, and a gas gauge that never moved even when it should have registered empty. Many ghosts accompanied me—I had not yet realized the true impossibility of abandoning one's history—but that trip was my life's great migration, the bridge between what was and all I hoped for.

My first destination was Phoenix, where I stayed with my good friend Cyd. It was December of 1981; the country was in a severe recession and work prospects were bleak. I talked to people in hotels and offices, people who were fortunate because they had jobs, who were powerful only because they might hold a clue or give a blessing. One of them actually smirked. He worked for the city and sat at a desk. He wore a polyester blazer and a cheap-looking tie and said lots of people would like to quit their lives back east and come to Arizona, lots of people.

I ran solo laps at a high school track in Tempe, running round and round as the sun sank down behind the bleachers. I ate too much trail mix and carrot cake. I received a deferment on my student loan, a citation for going forty in a school zone, and angry letters from family members who felt I had abandoned them. I didn't dare admit yet that things weren't working out. Another friend, Mary Ellen, invited me to stay with her in San Diego, so I figured I'd go the rest of the way to California, where at least I could look at the sea. "You're very brave," someone said. I knew that wasn't true.

I drove through the desert in my trusty green Buick, stopping at a stand along the highway to buy a tiny pair of turquoise earrings while big trucks rumbled by.

It was Groundhog Day, 1982 when I first rolled into California. I promptly set forth on a series of discouraging interviews and inquiries, and finally drove a bit further north on the Interstate 5 to see about a job in Orange County, despite its general reputation among the sun-bleached surf-watching stoners I met in Ocean Beach as a life-sucking vortex of crowded freeways, business parks, and other atrocities, all of which to me implied potential for employment. I was hired for a two-year, grant-funded improvisational position at a transportation agency in Santa Ana, where by chance there also worked a fellow named Monte who would soon become the best part of my saga. Remember that broken gas gauge I mentioned? I famously ran out of gas on the freeway one afternoon, managed to pull over onto the shoulder, and was teetering along in a silk blouse, tight skirt and high heels with a gas can in my hand when Monte happened to drive by. He was a welcome sight indeed, not on a white steed but in a white VW bus, and he rescued me that day. We stayed together.

By the time the jacaranda trees along Broadway had shed their petals like lavender snow and the hills of the Irvine Ranch had grown yellow with mustard and the Santa Anas were unleashing crazy cacophonies of wind chimes and making tall palms sway, I was a California woman. The decades flickered by.

Sometimes it seems I was always leaving, even from the start, and I am thankful for whatever angels were watching over me, for the kindness that carried me, for the stars that lit my way. I have reached a wondrous, implausible now…and maybe I should simply relax into it, marveling at the sky and the wren's song in the morning. But my past is restive lately, and I can't help but look back from my precarious little boat, still trying to figure things out, not returning but yearning to know and understand.

THERE. THEN.

What Happened In The Alley

When I was a kid, I wandered the streets, and sometimes I was solo. It was a different era, and although I suppose danger always lurked, we were given free rein, armed with a few basic rules such as crossing at the corner and never getting into a stranger's car. There were of course no cell phones, so an emergency dime was a good idea, but ten cents could also buy two candy bars, which was a very tempting transaction. The neighborhoods usually hummed with children—running, exploring, making up adventures—but there were also plenty of crabby grandmothers with their elbows on the window sills, looking out with nosy vigilance, ready to wag a finger and scold, and they wielded real authority.

My best friend Carol and I liked to talk to grown-ups—shopkeepers, mostly, or the man who fixed the traffic light, or a friendly fellow named Albert who was probably in his early thirties. Albert was the one who raised my father's eyebrow when I mentioned him in passing. "Who is this Albert?" he wanted to know, and he was not satisfied with my description of a nice-looking joke-telling man with a pencil-thin mustache much like his. "Why is he hanging around talking to little girls?" he asked. I had just assumed that Albert liked our company, but in my father's voice I heard a joy-killing sort of dissonance.

There were sinister things out there, just beneath the surface, about which I probably didn't really want to know.

And then a scary thing did happen. I was eight or nine and walked ten blocks each morning to Public School 179, sometimes with my brothers, and sometimes by myself. On this particular morning I was alone. I'd left home earlier than usual and the neighborhood was quiet and empty. I liked the city in the mornings, when it was just rousing from sleep; kitchen lights were turning on, breakfasts were beginning, stores were still closed, and someone was sweeping off a walkway with a rhythmic swishing of broom.

I moved briskly out of habit, although I had plenty of time, enjoying the percussion of my own steps upon the sidewalk. I felt autonomous and substantial, a purposeful girl in a navy blue skirt who knew where she was going all on her own. I passed mailboxes and maple trees, rows of red brick apartment buildings, and two-family houses bordered by square hedges. Just beyond East Eighth Street I began to imagine the sound of another set of footsteps behind me.

"Maybe I'm being followed," I thought, "just like someone in a detective story." It was a fun idea and I pretended it was true. I hastened my pace and the steps behind me accelerated as well. At the very moment when I realized that the steps were not imaginary, I felt a firm hand against my back and was pushed and then pulled into the narrow alleyway between two buildings set far back from the street. All the pretending abruptly drained out of me, and with it my good sense and volition. How quickly I turned into nothing.

He was a dark haired man so ordinary in appearance that I cannot recall a single feature of his face. Now he held me against the side of one of the buildings. From within I heard water running through a pipe and the sustained low hum of something electrical. I recognized the reassuring noises of mundane morning routines beginning and noticed for the first time the omnipresent undercurrent of sound beneath the city even in its quiet times. I could feel the cold and rough of brick, and the alien pressure of the stranger's weight. There was a vague smell about him, maybe stale tobacco, and something that was dissonant and other, something nauseating, outside of my world, outside of a little girl's comprehension. He released his hold on me, and I could have run but I stood before him meek and baffled.

I held a small stack of schoolbooks and a pencil case with a tiny plastic nametag attached to the zipper. He turned the nametag toward him and read it. "Don't be afraid, Cynthia," he said, and I was sickened by the sound of my own name issuing from his lips. Now he reached into his trousers and through his fly thrust out a fleshy protrusion that he asked me to touch. It did not occur to me that this was his penis. Actually, penis may not have even been a word I knew yet, but I'd glimpsed what my brother had and it did not resemble this thing. Perhaps I was in denial, but in truth I think I simply failed to understand. Why would someone corner me and ask me to touch him unless he yearned for touch? Why would someone yearn for touch unless no one ever touched him? Why would no one ever touch him? One look at his freakish anatomy made it clear. I concluded that he was showing me a deformed and swollen thumb so repulsive to others that he had to coerce random humans to touch it.

So this was the modus operandi of a tormented and mutated man—walk the early morning streets, drag some unsuspecting soul into an alley, and procure the longed-for feel of skin on skin. For an instant I almost felt pity. But no, that can't be true. More likely I was protecting myself from my terror and revulsion by inventing a story less threatening than the one I had been dragged into, the one I had no words for and could not begin to understand.

And yet I could not be the one to touch it. Alarms were going off inside my head. There was something very wrong. He took my hand and tried to guide it towards him, and I remained frozen with fear like a dumb animal, an easy victim. Suddenly there were new sounds as a door opened and slammed and a middle-aged man carrying a briefcase emerged and casually walked down the stairs at the front of the building, mere yards away from where I stood. I opened my mouth to yell for help but my voice was lodged in my throat and not a sound came out. I was a mute and paralyzed creature, forever suspended in a sickening tableau with a stranger whose intents were terrible and creepy. The man with the briefcase went on his way and the stranger turned towards me.

All at once God reappeared, giving me a shove, or maybe it was just belated instinct finally kicking in. My will returned and I yanked myself away and ran as fast as my skinny legs could carry me the entire distance to school where no one had yet gathered, but I touched the chain link playground fence as though it were home base. Later I sat in Mrs.

Olinger's fourth grade classroom doing arithmetic and spelling, and I didn't tell anyone what had happened.

We were all running a risk, I guess, and learning to navigate, learning to notice, learning that the world was bountiful and wondrous but we could not lean back into it with reckless abandon. There were signs to be deciphered, situations to avoid, intuitive knowledge to recognize and respect. I knew even then that I'd been spared not because I was smart, but because I was lucky, and that not all grown-ups would look out for me. Safety, I saw, was a relative term and I had a role in creating it.

One afternoon several months later, instead of going home when school was out, I walked alone to the Woolworth's on Flatbush Avenue, a completely different route that did not lead towards home. Nobody knew I was doing this, but our class was having a plant fair, whatever that means, and we were all supposed to bring plants to the classroom so we could take care of them and watch them flourish. I did not yet have a plant, so I intended to buy one at Woolworth's, which in those days was an emporium of earthly goods, from green plants to goldfish to goggles and games, and the rest of the alphabet too. I carried a quarter, and for fifteen cents I bought a tiny ivy plant in a tiny plastic pot.

But I must have lingered too long in Woolworth's, with all its colorful distractions, because when I stepped outside it had grown dark and everything looked different. Some of the stores were already beginning to close, and even Flatbush Avenue seemed quiet. I started to walk, holding my little ivy plant, and I turned down one of the side streets that would take me back towards Coney Island Avenue. All I saw were shadows, and I felt a sudden sense of fear. I had walked these streets many times with my mother, but now I wasn't even sure if I was headed in the right direction.

I still had that dime. I hurried back to Woolworth's, went into the phone booth at the front of the store and dialed my house. My father answered and I started to cry. "Stay where you are," he said. "I'll be there in a few minutes."

I watched for him through the big plate glass window that faced out onto Flatbush Avenue. A neon sign flickered on across the street. Headlight beams passed. Finally his familiar car pulled up to the curb, he stepped outside, and I ran into his arms. "I'm glad you had the good sense to call me," he said, hugging me tight. And I felt safe and loved and grateful.

I didn't know why I was crying so hard.

Reclamation

He was mine once, and he completed me. I loved his cheery, unflappable demeanor, his unblinking gaze, the mouth that never ceased to smile. There was pink in his cheeks, a perkiness to his little black nose, and dignity in his widow's peak, even if his hairline was a bit high. The four-fingered yellow-gloved hands hanging passively by his side were forever empty and unclenched, and he held his arms in a way that suggested a willingness to be hugged. He was a little bit squishy without being plump, and he had long ago lost his clothing but was self-possessed even in his underpants.

I certainly didn't think of it this way at the time, but this rubber Mickey Mouse seemed to have attained a state of spiritual enlightenment. Yes, he was Buddha-like, and if I didn't exactly rub his belly, I certainly enjoyed giving him a squeeze now and then, because that released a small and satisfying squeak. I realized that he was a baby-toy, and I didn't tote him around in public, but I liked knowing he was there. Was that so wrong?

Here's the awful part. When I had attained the advanced age of eight and had been Mickey's owner for as long as I could remember, I came home one day to discover him gone. In an impulsive gesture of munificence that at the same time underscores the difficulties my family had with concepts such as boundaries, privacy, and personal possession, my mother had given my Mickey away to a three-year-old boy who lived next door. I was outraged and heartbroken. "How *dare* you?" I sobbed.

My mother was genuinely surprised. She hadn't known how much I loved that rubber Mickey Mouse. No one did. Not even me. In fact, it is quite possible that the theft of him and the giving away of him are what transformed the small glow of my affection into a veritable conflagration. My heart welled with unprecedented passion for the beloved Mickey Mouse toy.

"I didn't realize you still played with the thing," my mother said. Of course her words only made me angrier, because even then I suspected there might be some protocol involving inquiries made to the owner before transferring an item to someone else. I suspected, too, that generosity with another person's belongings did not carry as many points in God's book of genuine good deeds. And I knew for sure that my mother, a legendary hoarder, was generally quite resistant to giving things away; I wondered what had come over her and why it had to happen with Mickey. *My* Mickey. In short, I was inconsolable. My tears and frustration escalated as the melodrama fed on itself.

Even so, I was willing to let the drama play out, as it usually did, in the privacy of our home, where volatility was the norm, and eventually it would have all whimpered away. But now my mother did the next awful thing: she telephoned the mother of the little boy next door and told her that I was terribly upset and wanted my rubber Mickey Mouse back.

Oh, she gave it back to me, all right. She knocked on the door, Mickey in tow, and asked to speak to me directly. "I thought you were a much nicer girl than this," she said, "and I thought you were a big girl, but here's your baby-toy back, and you've taken it away from a little boy, and I hope you're happy." I wasn't happy at all.

I took back the Mickey Mouse, but all I felt was embarrassment and shame, and he looked at me with his blank, benign eyes, and smiled his meaningless smile. I squeezed him half-heartedly and the little squeak sounded pathetic. He had lost his Buddha-esque ability to calm and cheer me, and it suddenly seemed he should belong to someone else. He had been my very first toy, or the first I could remember, and when I was a child, I thought as a child, but when I became a big girl, I put away childish things.

And who knows? Maybe the gap in me that never goes away has something to do with my abruptly truncated relationship with Mickey Mouse. Which might explain the weird elation I experienced when I saw him lying in a display case at a local thrift store just the other day. I asked the white-haired woman behind the counter if I could hold him for a moment.

"Oh, yes," she said, "vintage 1950's."

I told her that long ago I'd owned one just like it, and I had loved it very dearly.

"Twenty dollars," said the lady. "You can have him again."

I declined.

He was a rubber Mickey, nothing more. I pictured myself bringing him home, stuffing him into a drawer somewhere, just to know I owned him. I couldn't see the point of it. Who needs another object to remind us what's been lost? I knew I could never reclaim it.

The Kensington Kids

One day in 1960, I went to the birthday party of a classmate named Janet Fechner who lived near McDonald Avenue in Brooklyn, not far from my grandfather's pizzeria. Janet was visually memorable for her long blonde hair, which she wore pulled tightly back from her forehead and plaited into a single and substantial braid, a braid with true heft. At the party, I met her grandmother, who seemed an aged and shrunken replica of Janet herself, right down to the braid, now silver-gray. In my memory, we are standing outdoors by a sunlit walkway, and I am talking to the grandmother, who is originally from Norway, and she is telling me that as a young girl she used to waltz among the fjords, and I picture her in a white summer frock, dancing, and all around her is Norway, a mythical blue-green land that I decide then and there I will one day visit.

This may or may not have happened. That's the problem with memory, especially after fifty years' worth of metamorphosis, and especially when it starts with the dewy and dreamlike perspective of a child. Countless new layers of interpretation, alteration, and forgetting eventually distort or bury the experience and its facts, leaving behind a residue of fragmented stories. My head is full of these, and whether or not they actually happened, they have become my history.

I've been pondering this a lot ever since the curious phenomenon of Facebook deposited a handful of people onto my computer screen who were present in the long ago time and place of my childhood. These people are not family members, thus not tangled up in *that* peculiar and particular universe. They're just former classmates from the Kensington School, which we generally referred to as P.S. 179. Some of them actually *knew* Janet-with-the-yellow-braid.

It's odd to be in contact with folks who can recall tangible things I thought I alone remembered or validate details that had begun to seem dubious, including my own existence in this context. Like characters in some murky version of *Rashomon*, they offer observations I somehow missed, and perspectives different from my own, and collectively we can, if not quite reconstruct a history (and what would be the point?), at least browse through it. Our generation did not have adults with video cameras documenting every element of our lives; photographs from ordinary days are scarce enough to elicit the surprise of recognition and amazement that some random moment was preserved. We peer deeply into these pictures when they are posted, looking for clues about who we were and the textures of our lives. We marvel at cursive script on a chalkboard, the façade of a once-familiar building, and the faces of children now in their sixties, some of whose names we can still recall. We remember sitting in rows of wooden desks that still had inkwells, dressing up for Friday assemblies in boy and girl versions of white shirts and little red ties, being labeled early and conspicuously as smart or dumb, good or trouble. Teachers were strict in those days, and we kids generally accepted our plight and seldom communicated with each other about the whole weird epic of grammar school while it was happening to us. Now suddenly we're comparing notes.

Steve, one of my newfound Facebook friends from Mrs. Olinger's fourth grade class, remembers wearing a bright yellow badge in sixth grade that proclaimed him a monitor. "I served my school during lunch as the monitor of the north gate facing East Third Street," he wrote. "Ah, the great feeling of power, bullying the younger kids and being closest to the ice cream truck! Until I got busted for selling firecrackers…so much for the entrepreneurial spirit."

As for me, I never attained such heights of authority or nerve. Mostly I kept my head down and tried to please, although I did once get into an all-out fistfight in the schoolyard with another girl (whose name I dare not mention, now that I realize so many of these people are real and still out there). I remember a frenzy of scratching, punching, pinching, and notebook throwing, with both of us down on the ground while a circle of kids excitedly gathered around us, and I guess I won, because the girl picked up her books and ran away. Then a boy named Michael, who had never before noticed me, came up and said, "Hurray for the victor!" I felt sick.

Fran, who was also in Mrs. Olinger's class and now lives in Calabasas, California, recently went back to our old neighborhood, Brooklyn's zip code 11218, and posted new pictures of the school and other landmarks. "What a flashback!" wrote Carol, yet another of our cohorts, after seeing a picture of the brooding brick building that is still P.S. 179. "I lived right down the block and passed it a million times."

A photograph of the basement area that was used for indoor recess and hot lunch prompted recollections about the games we played on that green tiled floor, getting in line to trudge up the stairs to our classrooms, the smells of tomato soup, rain, and radiator steam. We remembered Hurricane Donna, and crouching under our desks in anticipation of nuclear attacks, and Mitchell-who-died-by-drowning, (although as Fran pointed out, there was not a counselor in sight to help us through our various traumas), and a rocket launch viewed on a tiny black and white television screen set up on the stage in the auditorium. Mostly, we remembered Brooklyn as it was, and we remembered with fondness: candy stores, pickles in barrels, railroad flats on Ocean Parkway or Coney Island Avenue.

"A blast from the past," said Barry, another Kensingtonian, in an email, "...or is it just a long dream that never ends?" It does feel like a dream, and that's what makes it so startling: one doesn't expect to hear from people who dreamed the same strange dream or were right there with you in yours. It injects a bit of otherness into what has been for so long a personal and individualized possession. And although I barely knew most of these folks even in the old days and have very little concept of who they are today, it seems to me we went through something big and formative together, and are thus forever linked. I feel a certain kinship with these Kensington kids.

There was even some talk among us about trying to find Janet Fechner. But what if we did? And what if I then learned that I'd never been to any birthday party at her house? What if it turned out that her grandmother had died long before Janet was born and wasn't Norwegian at all? Would I have to revise the little vignette I have owned for all these years?

Never.

It brings to mind the work of Patricia Hampl, who has written extensively on memoir and how invention inevitably permeates any personal narrative. "Memory," she says, "is not a warehouse of finished stories, not a gallery of framed pictures." Much of what we recall is colored by our own imagination, and even if we set out to write down what we think we know, it is often through the process of writing that we actually *discover* what we know. Intentionality, Hampl reminds us, does not run the show—intuition does, and heart.

Something Janet's grandmother told me at that long ago party, whatever the words she used, gave to me the fjords of Norway, a waltz in a white dress, and some implicit sense that everything was both poignant and possible. It's a private space in the co-op dream, and it's unconfirmed, but I've kept it all this time, and regardless of the facts, it still rings true.

On Coney Island Avenue

May was a haggard-looking woman and Cookie her thin pale little daughter. I haven't uttered their names since 1958, and their whereabouts and outcomes are unknown, but they lived two doors away from us on Coney Island Avenue. Sometimes in the night the walls of those apartments seemed to tremble, and neighbors heard the yelling and crying from within. Doors slammed, chairs banged, the air was filled with curses and muffled pleas. In the morning, May would hurry down the street, head down, clasping Cookie's small hand in hers. "He showed up again last night," the neighbors would say. Here's to May and Cookie, and I hope Cookie's life turned out better than its start.

And here's to miserable Mrs. Milicci, elbows on a pillow at the windowsill, monitoring the happenings on the street with a constant scowl, mother of eleven kids but licensed to scold anyone in sight, readily meddling in Italian-accented English. "I saw your father with a woman the other day," she shouted to me once. "She wasn't your mother." I thought about the earring with the purple stone I'd found on the floor of my father's car, like a tiny star dropped carelessly from the galaxy where laughter may have lived, and I was fine not knowing whose or why or if.

Here's to the old woman who walked the avenue, muttering to herself, looking for coins on the sidewalk or bottles with deposit to redeem. Newly Sunday-schooled, my best friend Carol Bessey and I tried to befriend her once. We said hello and asked her what her name was. "Leave me alone, you little bastards!" she replied.

And here's to Harry Nathanson, the kindly grocer, who gave us credit via handwritten IOUs he slipped into the cash register drawer, who trusted and was always paid. He kept a good store: wooden floors, canned goods lined up tidily, milk in glass bottles, Dixie cups of ice cream, bags of Wise potato chips, even a display area where you could vote for Miss Rheingold as often as you liked. Here's to crabby Mr. Gluck as well, who ran the corner candy store, source of sodas and comics and ice cream cones with sprinkles, a place where you felt filthy rich if you had three nickels in your hand.

And to Mr. Herman, who repaired and sold clocks...a whole store filled with clocks and nothing else, some of them cuckoo or tall stately grandfathers, and Mr. Thorner, whose trade was nails and hardware, I suppose, but who mostly sat outside smoking his cigar. And Mr. Keating, who might buy ice cream for everyone when the Good Humor truck came by, and Winnie Smith, always walking with a pair of pug-nosed dogs. And a humble nod to the tailor and his wife, on whose arms were etched the tattooed numbers of a concentration camp.

Here's to Charlotte, the white-haired lady around the corner who always said good morning and along whose chain link fence marigolds grew. And here's to our enemy, Francis, the boy who lived near the tailor shop; I don't know why we were at war. Here's to Carol's Aunt Marie, who took us in a rowboat once on the lake at Prospect Park, and Charlie-the-butcher, who gave us slices of bologna wrapped in sturdy paper when we came for trick or treat. And to Ivan, who kissed me quickly on a hot bright day, paused at a storefront, everything glaring and yellow-gold and I was nine years old and knew I didn't like him that way, but we were pretty good friends.

Here's to the jump ropers and hopscotch players, the hide and seekers, the dandelion pickers, the sore losers, the dirt bomb hurlers, and the great pretenders who could turn the street into anything we wanted it to be.

Here's to rain on the sidewalk, popsicle stick boats set sail in gutter streams, stoops and rooftops and summer nights. Here's to beauteous strands of spoken Italian, Yiddish accents, Irish grins.

Here's to the people who live there today, new groups of hopefuls finding their way.

Il Linguaggio Segreto
(The Secret Language)

My grandfather Raffaele had a bungalow someplace, but all I can remember of it is a triangle of sunlight and faded sea green walls and the curlicue cadence of the words that it held. He and my father spoke Italian. They talked in the tempo of the south, a fervent and volatile kind of speech whose words never ended flat but spun in capricious dances through the air and concluded on magnificent mellifluous vowels. It was a sumptuous, sun-drenched language, and in its passionate rhythms I intuitively understood the punchy ardors of life. I wished my tongue would know this dance, wondered what the secrets were that could only be expressed in such a way.

The English Grandpa spoke to me came out in coarsely broken pieces that did not reflect his soul. Truth was, he didn't speak to me much at all, but I watched him closely and I felt connected to him in a fundamental way I did not understand. I have a photograph of him taken at a beach, and even on the sand, he is wearing loose trousers, light straw loafers, a white shirt with the sleeves rolled up slightly, and a tie. He had the dapper look of a European gentleman, although he was built like the peasant he was, stocky and short, and was even missing a tooth or two. His hands were strong and his nails uncut, and even through his seventies, his hair was black but for a grey patch at each temple.

Raffaele had come to America at the age of seventeen on a two-masted steamer called the *Citta di Torino*, arriving at Ellis Island on July 13, 1905. He had left behind a stone house, a small good field of rich volcanic earth, and three brothers whose aging children I would one day meet, many years later, in Boscoreale. That tattered Italian village could not contain his husky dreams, although it held his heart forever.

Life in the new country was hard, but Grandpa was too proud to write home about defeats and disappointments. Letters from the brothers went unanswered as he painted the walls of the RKO theater, ran the Eden Pizzeria on McDonald Avenue, bet on the horses, and occasionally speculated in real estate, though he always had to sell too soon and too cheaply. My brother Eddie and I used to wait for him in his little real estate office in Canarsie, fascinated by a safe that he told us held countless thousands of dollars—if only he hadn't lost the combination. As he worked undisturbed at his desk and checked the names of good race prospects in the *Daily News*, we persistently experimented with different numbers and various twists of the dial. The safe of course remained sealed, and the three of us always went home penniless.

At various times, both my father and my grandfather worked as painters. Grandpa had learned art techniques from *his* father in Boscoreale. He made elegant charcoal drawings of faces and figures, a fine craft that eventually metamorphosed into broad-brush house painting in the interest of survival. Daddy's specialty was murals and decorative art—he painted Roman ruins and leafy boughs, and could make a surface look like marble or wood grain. The walls of our house were the canvas upon which he practiced, and so I grew up amidst peacocks, clowns, exotic flowers, and a general effect called "splitter splatter" which was created by hitting a hammer on the handle of a wet paintbrush at just the right distance from the wall. Sometimes Grandpa and Daddy worked together with Vito Plantamura, who respectfully called my father "Buss". Along with my Uncle Joey, they had an interest in a place called the Marlin Hotel in St. Petersburg, Florida, which they renovated in the 1950s and then sold.

The Eden Pizzeria was the Grandpa venture I remember best; I could easily walk there after school and often did. In its storefront window my grandfather created a veritable jungle of plants in large olive oil tins with punctured holes for drainage. When the sunlight slanted through the grimy glass, the leaves became luminous, and the splendid tins with their Italian names were gilded and shiny. My favorite plant was one whose slender leafy hands closed whenever I touched them. Grandpa said they were *sensitivo*—and he called this the sensitive plant. I never learned its true botanical name, but many years later, I found its timid sisters growing wild in Florida, recoiling at my touch, or perhaps my silly, excited squeals.

Pizza at Raffaele's shop cost fifteen cents a slice, and although this was substantial change, I would not accept my pizza for free. I shyly put my coins down on the white Formica counter as though I were an ordinary customer and waited for the warm slice, served up on wax paper. I loved its bubbly crust and stretchy strings of chewy mozzarella. Unfortunately, Grandpa thought pizza was fine for other kids, but for his own grandchildren it was never as good as the oily fish he had just baked in a pan, or the cooked escarole, or the hard crusty bread from the oven, and more often than not, these became my lunch.

Food was a serious matter with Grandpa. Once a week, he would drive his faded green station wagon to the farmer's market before daybreak to get first choice of the very best produce. He sought and found perfection in tomatoes. He gathered dandelion greens and put them in salads. He brought back sweet firm plums, small tender artichokes, and fresh fish from Sheepshead Bay tidily wrapped in newspaper. Olive oil was essential to all cooking; it was years before I realized that other kinds of oil existed. And bread was not bread if the crust provided no resistance to the teeth.

I saw my grandfather as an emissary from a faraway land, and the colorful remnants of his culture appealed to me greatly. But I did not believe it was possible to truly know him without knowing his language. I asked my father to teach me Italian, and he helped me memorize a sentence or two, but it was only a game. "You can learn someday," he said, "but it's not important now. In this world, English is the key, and you must concentrate on that." So I simply listened from the silent outskirts to conversations that seemed ornate, tumultuous, and lush with mystery.

But sometimes my heart had a way of translating. There was anger between Grandpa and my father, as well as a stilted and powerful love. How else to explain the raised voices, the snap and spit of shortened words, the palpable, familiar pain? Childhood had not been easy for the sons of Raffaele, for he was often gone, and his wife

Assunta, to whom he had been untrue, was a saintly suffering woman. She sat at her window on Coney Island Avenue, knowing all the sad truths, as such women do. When she died, Grandpa married his mistress, a woman named Rose. Daddy never forgot these misplaced loyalties, but the gnarled bond between father and son endured. He often brought Grandpa jars of homemade lentil soup, and in the late afternoon, he would secretly place a small sweaty stack of dollar bills into the cash register at the pizzeria.

Only once did I have time alone with my grandfather. It was July 17, 1954, the day my sister was born. My parents were at the hospital, and I don't know where my brothers were, but I became Grandpa's charge for an afternoon. He took me to the Brooklyn Botanical Gardens, and a more enchanting place did not exist anywhere. We walked through a greenhouse together, where the air was moist and tropical, and fragrant in a way I had never known. I remember a ruckus of green and yellow parrots from the palms and rubber trees, though I am sure there were none, and a wooden footbridge over a clear pond into which glinting pennies had been tossed for wishing. It is as though we took a journey together to some South American dream, just my grandfather and me. And to this day, I cannot enter a greenhouse without thinking of him, nor can I see one without entering.

Those summer days of childhood were served to me in thick sun-buttered slices, and anything was possible. I never doubted that I would learn Italian, never believed there was a single thing I would not do if I chose it. I loved the smells of paint and housework, for these held promise. I loved the fruits of earth, and kitchen sounds, for these were life's comforts. But discord was my native tongue, for nothing ever seemed to settle and end right. Watching the struggles of my grandfather and my father, I braced myself for battle, believing that my life would be better, but not without a fight. In the meantime, there was lemon ice in pleated cups beneath the el and rain puddles full of neon light.

When my grandfather moved away to Florida, summer had ended, and there was no good-bye. The New York winters had always been mean, and his various endeavors and speculations were becoming harder to sustain. He would live near Uncle Joey in St. Petersburg. He would have a garden. It was the right decision for him. But within two years, he had a stroke. He lingered for a week. Uncle Joey's daughter stayed at his bedside and spoke to him gently, as I wished I could have done.

And so on a gray day in February 1965, I sat in the back of a funeral parlor in Brooklyn incongruously doing my chemistry homework. I could not comprehend the casket within view that held my grandfather's body, so I lowered my head and tended to my textbook as though it were more important than anything. I could hear Rose wailing, and there were strands of Italian entwined with English, punctuated by sobs. My own feelings were twisted into a terrible knot and I seemed to have no voice. I had never told my grandfather that I loved him. There were so many things that had not been said, so many things I would never know.

But my grandfather came back to me in dreams. He gave me a gypsy ring with ruby stones, and he spoke to me in an eloquent wordless language that I effortlessly understood. He visited me many times, and he always returned in the winter to bring me the sunlight and warmth of greenhouses, gardens, and southern Italy. He had begun a journey in 1905 and reached the eastern shore. It was for me, he said, to continue, and I have. He gave me his trust and his yearning. He told me about work, which is good in itself. He told me about love—fierce, irrational, and everlasting. And he told me about outrageous hope that can stare down anything and never blink, hope that is born and reborn in a thousand incarnations. And I knew the secret language then, and I hugged him through his overcoat and time.

Hiding

What do you think I'd see
If I could walk away from me

Lou Reed

Once when I was little I hid in the hallway closet and waited for my absence to be noted. I crouched there, listening to the rise and fall of voices and assorted household sounds until I began to feel oddly disconnected from all of the muffled commotions. The familiar world outside grew strange, and as my eyes adjusted to the darkness, the forms of brooms and jackets seemed comforting. The closet was my habitat. I nodded off. When the door abruptly opened, I was like an alien creature blinking into the light, suddenly cornered and exposed. My inexplicable presence gave quite a fright to the opener of the door, of course, and there was reproach instead of welcome. But I only wanted someone to have missed me.

Another time, I hid out of boredom, or maybe it was spite. I had gone with my mother to a resort in the Catskill Mountains, a region we referred to as "the country". These annual expeditions occurred in the summers of my childhood for a period of several years; I was not at all fond of them and wished I didn't always have to be my mother's escort. We would say good-bye to my father at the Port Authority, take Trailways to Kingston, where we ate sandwiches on the bus while it sat parked for a time, and then go on to Ellenville or Palenville or some other small upstate town. It was a long ride and evoked the feeling not of vacation but exile.

When we arrived, someone from the hotel would pick us up at the bus stop (which might be just a little general store or filling station) and drive us to a large old wooden house with a front porch and smelly guest rooms. There was a structure nearby for parties and dancing that was glamorously referred to as the casino, a cluster of small separate bungalows, and a dining hall to which we were summoned by the clanging of a bell. I remember the most peculiar details, such as the fact that the milk was served in icy bottles with cream at the top, and there were rusty metal lawn chairs that tipped over easily, and the rooms we stayed in had big empty dressers and lumpy mattresses.

Occasionally I found a friend my age in the country, and I tried to make the best of things, but in truth I felt sad and strange the whole time I was there. One afternoon while my mother was napping I stared into the murky dresser mirror, entranced by the fine lines of scratches in its silvery surface, and by my own shadowy face within, like looking into a well. Then I impetuously cut my hair, adding brand new wispy bangs for a needed change of mood. My mother, who did not believe I had jurisdiction over my head, took one horrified look and yelled at me so long that Marcella, the owner's daughter, came upstairs and knocked at the door to see if I was okay. She came bearing gifts, too: a clear plastic purse with a Three Musketeers bar inside. (That, and her obvious sympathy, made the ordeal almost worthwhile. My sobbing ceased with a mouthful of chocolate.)

Now you have a sense, though, of the context in which my ultimate hiding caper occurred. I don't recall if I planned it deliberately or if it was just another of my whims, but I wandered into the front room of the big house and sat behind a plump armchair, my legs stretched out before me underneath the chair, and I stayed there for what felt like hours. I listened to my mother's initial inquiries about my whereabouts, then observed how her voice rose gradually into tones of worry, alarm, and even panic. Somehow I'd thought this was between the two of us, but suddenly others were being solicited to help hunt for me, and my name was on everyone's lips. Finally some eagle-eyed guest spotted my saddle shoes beneath the chair. Once again I was greeted with reprimand, well deserved.

I was a mother myself before I fully understood the cruelty of this hiding business. I'm sure that every parent knows those moments of panic when you lose sight of your child for an instant in a department store, for example, or some other potentially perilous place. As a four-year-old, my own daughter and her friend Seychelle decided to hide under the bed in our house when Seychelle's mother Sonja came to pick her up. We lived in a place about as safe and idyllic as one could imagine, a trailer park on the north end of Laguna Beach, but suddenly I had visions of predators driving through the rows ready to pull little girls into their cars.

Sonja and I scanned the street, calling their names again and again, our irrational anxiety mounting. The girls seemed to be missing for a long time, though perhaps it was only ten minutes or so. When the little duo emerged sheepishly from the bedroom, it was my daughter who explained: "We were afraid to come out. The more worried you sounded, the madder you were going to be, and the scared-er we got. But then we started to be afraid of how long we were going to have to stay under there."

"We were getting hungry too," added Seychelle. It sounds funny now. Even back then, it didn't take too long for us to laugh. Maybe my daughter remembers it differently.

But all of this is ancient history. In my life today, hiding takes on a different meaning. It is the peculiar freedom of being no longer young, of passing unnoticed, of accepting the fluidity of things and inevitable disappearance. While memory fills me up, time is also dissolving me. I feel small and plain and close to the ground, and I no longer hide in the hope of being found, but in the hope of finding.

The Babysitter

Before I got my first real job—as a check-out girl two evenings a week and all-day Saturday in the Big Apple supermarket on Wheeler Road, the place where I learned to hate work—I had another gig: babysitting. It was suburban Long Island, mid-1960s, and all around us woods were being cleared to make way for rows of new houses as people fled the city, bringing children and giving birth to new ones. And so, while the times they were a'changing, I was wiping noses and peering into neighbors' lives behind the scenes. I didn't mind.

In fact, I thought it was cool, especially on New Year's Eve, when folks would come home liquored and magnanimous and you could make as much as six or seven bucks. My friend Rae had the dream gig with a stylish woman named Thomasina, who acted like every night was New Year's Eve, and never failed to provide ice cream, not to mention bags of expensive hand-me-down clothing. I once accepted a sitting job for Thomasina's sister Liv—Rae had already committed to Thomasina that night—and I approached it with greedy hopes, but it turned out Liv was surly and cheap, not at all like her sister. It worked out all right; I don't recall a thing about the children involved, but Rae and I talked on the phone most of the night, comparing notes and gossiping and freaking each other out with scary stories and imagined noises. (That's what babysitters often did for amusement in those days; when they weren't sneaking in their boyfriends, they liked to freak each other out.)

I didn't need Liv, anyway. I had my own turf, and I was in demand, even on school nights. It seemed that all the mothers on Long Island, whether married or divorced, were ready to step out, leaving the kiddies behind, and I was a rare gem—a responsible teen-age girl, experienced as a big sister, and genuinely desperate for coins, so desperate, in fact, that the pay, which was fifty cents an hour, was a reasonable incentive to say yes. That yes meant that I would not only watch the kids…in an active, *let-me-entertain-you* way…but also clean up any dishes or mess left behind in the grown-up's haste to escape, get the children ready for bed and into it, and then spend hours in bleak living rooms waiting.

Unfortunately, I was never able to sleep on someone's couch, and in those days of three working television channels that eventually sputtered into late-night nothingness, TV was no distraction. I usually did my homework, little drudge that I was, then watched the clock, my only consolation being that every full sixty-minute sweep would mean an additional fifty cents in my wallet. It was not beyond me, either, to contemplate my surroundings with an unwarranted sense of superiority and dismay, all the still-new ticky-tacky houses with their Sears Roebuck furniture and matched lamps on side tables and utterly oppressive ordinariness. I would peek nosily into drawers and flip through address books by the telephone and search the fridge and cupboards for anything worth eating. There was a hunger behind all the soda pop and breakfast cereals, a kind of emptiness amidst the middle-class possessions, perhaps not even paid for. With the arrogance of a teen-age girl, I judged, and I concluded that *I* would do it all differently someday.

I had two clients who most frequently called. My favorite was a redheaded divorcee who drove a red sports car. She was usually still getting dressed when I came over, and when she stepped out, her red lipstick newly applied, her outfit carefully chosen, she invariably looked glamorous. She had one child, a little boy named Tommy, whom she hugged tightly and sadly every time she left. She seemed almost guilty about leaving, like it was something she had to do but didn't really want to, and it was clear to me she was trying to find a new father for Tommy, but Tommy might have preferred just to spend more time with her. The scent of her perfume would linger in the air for hours afterward, and Tommy and I would sit on the couch side-by-side, and I would read him stories in the cloud of his mother's fragrance, and gradually he'd grow sleepy. This was an easy gig.

The other job, on the same street, was the Fusco family, a more complicated picture. It involved a married couple with two kids, a docile little girl and her brother who disliked me. The Fuscos liked the full-service aspects of my sitting business and took lavish advantage of my apparent willingness to wash their dirty dinner dishes. Once they left while the little girl had what appeared to be conjunctivitis, completely unattended, ignored, and unmentioned. She woke up in the night crying, her eyes swollen and crusted shut, and I somehow found what I needed to make a boric acid solution and wash her eyes and comfort her. I was fifteen years old. It seems amazing that I even knew to do that, but I was probably mimicking the way my father cared for us. Meanwhile, it was a school night, and they stayed out hours later than they had promised, and I was worried about how I would feel in the morning, and angry when they finally walked in. "Honey, you know you can just sleep on the couch," said Mrs. Fusco. "What's the difference?"

I guess that fifty cents an hour must have meant a lot to me, because I continued to accommodate their requests. One evening when I walked over to babysit, Mr. Fusco was not there, and Mrs. Fusco came to the door in a hideous pink dress, a lacy thing with a wide hoop skirt like a little girl's, and very short, revealing a pair of chunky legs that were frankly not her best asset. She wore high-heeled shoes as though to elevate the whole concoction, and had her black hair teased and lacquered into a tall beehive upsweep style. "I'll be meeting Frank there," said Mrs. Fusco, and off she went to wherever it was, her pink dress swishing.

Another long night awaited me. This may have been the time when the boy and I had it out, just as siblings might. "You're not my mother," he said, defying me when I asked him to go to bed. "I don't have to listen to you."

"Oh yes, you do," I said. Things escalated. Lest you think I was an angel, I may have called him a little shit or some other term of endearment. He may have said fuck you. There was some mutual shoving, shouting, a door slammed, tears. I don't remember how it ended, and I don't remember how the little girl reacted, but it was a singularly unpleasant night on the babysitting circuit.

At last the children were in bed and I waited. I waited until the midnight hour slipped into morning, and morning began to lighten the sky, and there was still no sign of the Fuscos. Finally, Mr. Fusco appeared, and he was alone. He did not appear to have dressed for the same occasion his wife had attended. He wore a white shirt, unbuttoned at the top, just regular office clothes, and he looked weary and disheveled and smelled vaguely of scotch. We went outside to his car so he could drive me home, two short blocks and turn a corner, five minutes perhaps—the kids would be fine.

All the houses dozed, shades drawn, front lawns dewy. A neighborhood cat blinked at us and slid away. I sat next to Mr. Fusco on the front seat and when we got to my driveway he turned for a moment and looked at me in a significant way, a way I didn't want to be looked at. "It's late," I said.

"You have no idea," he murmured, as I let myself out.

I didn't get paid, and I'd never go back to ask. I only knew that I was tired, and I'd had quite enough of babysitting.

Losing My Voice

My voice is not a reliable instrument. Maybe it's because there are so many voices inside my head, voices louder than mine, more certain of themselves. I was a child who sat in classrooms too shy to speak. If I needed to go to the bathroom, I endured the discomfort rather than ask. If I knew the answer to Mrs. Olinger's question, I held it in my mouth like a piece of hard candy. When a strange man pulled me into an alley way on my way to school, the scream I should have screamed remained lodged in my throat, and I stood for many seconds like a mute dumb animal until some rush of good sense pushed me and I ran. I never told a soul.

I had a long history of silenced voices. When she was a little girl, my mother sang like a nightingale until she was invited to audition for a radio show—it was to be her one big moment. She told me the story many years later. "I opened my mouth," she said, "and nothing came out." I could picture it: the small round empty O of her open mouth, the silent ride home, the unspeakable disappointment. I already knew that sinking sense of helplessness. I was a person who smiled stupidly in social situations and lived with an inability to navigate in a verbal world where clever people effortlessly chatted and sparred, where eloquent people moved others with

me out was always evidence to him of my good instincts. In his Old World view of life, only family mattered, but I yearned for acceptance in that outside world, and I'd seriously blown it. I dreaded going back to school on Monday, where I proved to be the subject of a few whispers and giggles in the corridor, but was quickly forgotten. Jack looked at me once with questions in his eyes and forevermore avoided me.

I had a special spot on my pillow that brought me good dreams, and I knew how dust danced in a shaft of sunlight, and how summer rain sounded when it pelted the oak leaves just outside my bedroom window. I could run fast and sometimes did, all alone in the cool of dusk. I had memorized a poem by T.S. Eliot about a man who heard the mermaids sing but did not think they sang for him, and I knew exactly how he felt: I lived among but apart, my music snow-silent, my true voice dormant, my heart forever heavy with its undelivered mail.

Forty Years Later I Get To Explain

If you're reading these stories in order, and no one says you must, you now know the very short story of my humiliating date with Jack in 1966. I saw him at school the following week, but we didn't acknowledge each other then, or ever, and I filed it away—just another painful adolescent memory. I trust we all have a collection of those.

But a few years ago, prompted by a discussion of "voice" at a South Coast Writing Project workshop, I wrote out the story and read it aloud to my colleagues. One teacher asked if she could read it to her high school students, certain that they could relate to it, despite the difference in our generations.

She was right. Even the coolest among them had their own experiences with shyness and awkwardness, with saying exactly the wrong thing or nothing at all, with feeling sort of paralyzed and stupid. They too had sometimes gotten lost in the gap between what they felt and what they outwardly expressed. But they wondered, also, how it might have seemed from Jack's point of view.

Hmmm. Can you imagine contacting a guy you dated (to use the term loosely) forty years earlier to ask him how he felt back then? Would he even remember me? But I figured I had nothing to lose. I'd try to find him and I'd do it in the guise of being a writer, and I'd do it for the kids, and I'd do it, truthfully, to finally close the loop on this embarrassing incident, retroactively explaining, and perhaps even redeeming myself.

Fast forward to the wonders of the web. He had an uncommon last name and had stayed on Long Island. I found him easily and sent an email. I asked him if he remembered me and our...um...date.

He certainly did. It turns out it was his first official date. Ever. Oh, dear. Here are a few of the things he said in the course of our brief email correspondence:

I remember thinking when I asked you out that you were beautiful, but afterwards I thought you were really in love with yourself, and what a bitch! It's funny—high school is such a weird time for mostly everyone. We are trying to figure things out with hormones flowing and bodies and minds growing. But I had such a great time in high school, I didn't want to graduate.

We certainly differ there.

He continued: *I'm sure I sulked and was perplexed for a week or so, but really there was always someone coming up saying 'guess who has a crush on you' and so you move on. However, it always stuck in the back of my mind. Was there more to it? Is it something I said? Did I smell? Though I was an upper classman I surely at that time was not as confident and sophisticated as you may have thought. I guess it was easier not to talk to each other after that date and just ignore it.*

In a subsequent message he added these thoughts: *My first thought was how conceited you were in those days, but deep down I had always hoped there was more to it, and I'm very happy to have heard from you. Don't be too remorseful about being shy in high school...most of us were....and as for our date, I was possibly almost as self-conscious and shy as you were, or I would have certainly made more of an attempt to initiate a conversation.*

Who knew?

Then he mused about our town: *I occasionally drive through Central Islip past my old house or St. John of God Elementary School to reminisce. Funny, most of our families couldn't rub two nickels together in those days. But I was happy, and life is grand.*

So he seemed like a nice guy back then, and he seems like a nice guy now. Before running out of things to say, we condensed the decades of our lives into a few key facts, compared notes about our grown-up children, and updated one another about friendships, marriages, and several deaths. Vietnam, AIDS, cancer...aren't we all just the stories of our generation?

When he sent me a photo, I was taken aback by the sight of a handsome white-haired gentleman, the sort you'd glimpse on a golf course, a grandfather type.

Then I remembered that I'm not sixteen either.

And he's right about our families. They never had much, but they worked hard and loved us fiercely, hoping always to give us better chances than they had known. It seems so far away and long ago, but out of all the infinite possibilities of time and place, we few were somehow thrown together, and it's fascinating to learn how the once overlapping stories have diverged and unfolded. We are the beneficiaries of such miraculous things.

A Place For Us

Long ago and in another life, Rae was my friend. As a matter of fact, she was my best friend, and I utterly adored her. She had a sense of mischief and adventure, a quick wit and a gritty voice, and a waif-like beauty that we all yearned to possess in those days, something along the lines of Marianne Faithfull. She was a person with charisma, although I wouldn't have known that word for it then, and I fell completely under her spell, always mildly amazed that she found my company at all appealing. It may well have been my worshipful devotion that appealed to her most of all, but it would be many years before I understood that.

Rae grew up in a clamorous ragtag family of eleven children. Her father, a thin man from Texas named Jordan Clarence, worked hard but spent a lot of time in a bar on Carlton Avenue. Her mother, a good Catholic woman of ample flesh and resounding voice, was hilariously eccentric and superstitious, but also full of love, and irrepressibly good-natured. Rae honed her survival skills and manipulative talents in this crowded, chaotic household, and the distracted parenting granted her an unusual amount of autonomy and freedom. She didn't have to sneak around as I did; she just came and went freely, and in the eyes of my over-protective Italian father, she was a very bad influence.

But most of our escapades were rather innocent. In summer, if I spent the night, we might sit for hours on her front stoop on Elmore Street talking about our hopes and schemes and flirting with the local cops who kept pulling over to chat. Sometimes we took walks along the railroad tracks and through the streets of the cheesy housing tracts of the town we couldn't wait to get out of, and once we discovered a secret wooded area by a creek beneath an overpass, where we ate chocolate-covered toffee bars and, corny as it sounds, we sang this song from *West Side Story*, and we sang it from the heart:

> *There's a place for us,*
> *Somewhere a place for us.*
> *Peace and quiet and open air*
> *Wait for us*
> *Somewhere.*

Rae and I dreamed of having boyfriends and made long chains out of gum wrappers the exact heights we imagined they'd be, chewing lots of Wrigley's spearmint and Juicy Fruit in the process—it was a fad among girls at that time. We bought cheap make-up in Woolworth's and practiced applying liquid eyeliner, curving it into exotic black wings or painting on lower lashes just like Twiggy's. Once we tried getting drunk together: Rae got sick and I couldn't manage more than a sip. (Our favorite drink was tea with milk and sugar.) For a while we went to mass on Sundays only because we knew a certain group of boys would be there, and afterwards we'd go hang out with them in some Lowell Avenue basement listening to music, so my father was right in his skepticism about my religious devotion, but honestly, nothing happened.

I think the worst thing we did was go to New York City without permission on a school night with our good friend Ron, a college guy who had a car, and there was hell to pay for that. But all we did in the city was walk around aimlessly, astonished to be there but trying to pretend we belonged. I have an enduring image of Rae that night, standing in front of a little grocery store in the Village, wearing a cotton print dress, very short, very 1960s, and biting into a large green apple. A man walked by and said, "That apple is bigger than you are!" and she smiled her heart-stopping smile, and he sighed. It's funny how an inconsequential moment like that can inhabit your head for more than forty years.

Rae got that sort of attention all the time—the airy banter reserved for the adorable. She was somehow both innocent and sexy back then, and she knew how to play it. I wanted to be like her, but I lacked the knack, not cute enough, or quick enough. So I followed her lead and basked in her reflected light, and I interpreted her occasional jabs as insights that might be good for me, convinced that she was deeper than most people realized. I saw that she could turn suddenly cold and was capable of grudges that calcified and never went away, but I focused on the fact that she was also very kind. She felt sorry for people, tried to intervene, turned them into projects for a while. I was probably a project more than once. My husband has concluded, based on the many anecdotes I've shared with him over the years, that she was a textbook example of the archetype we now refer to as Mean Girl, case closed.

But it's never that simple, is it? And I loved her with the intensity of love young girls have for their best friends. Even when we were miserable, if we were together, it was a dark and glamorous misery; it was theater. We walked through the rain in short black skirts and fishnet hose singing Bob Dylan songs and eating Twinkies because they resembled little sponge-cake coffins. We took pictures of each other posing in a graveyard, made up nonsense poetry and chanted it out loud, went to a Gene Pitney concert at the Commack Arena.

In the 1970s we took a cross-country drive in a Volkswagen bug, Rae and her then-husband bickering in the front, me in the back seat by the cooler. The seat was littered with soda cans and candy wrappers, like the inescapable debris of our past lives. We drove through Utah's red rock lunar landscapes and in Arizona detoured to get a quick look at the Grand Canyon, taking pictures with our plastic Instamatics. "Well, we've seen the Grand Canyon," said Rae afterwards, "and it's a big yawn." By then she was a sultry smoker, short denim shorts revealing skinny tan legs, her long hair sun-bleached. We were already nearing the end of our friendship but didn't know it yet.

And of course it didn't end well. I guess I disobeyed a rule, or overstepped my sidekick role. Do the details even matter? My life was a mess, but I was slowly and surely becoming myself, and in doing so, I fell seriously and irrevocably out of favor. "You're dead to me," Rae said, and never spoke a word to me again. I went to her house once; she looked right through me to the street beyond, and quietly closed the door. Believe me, it hurt at the time. And no one could understand it—we'd been good friends...*best* friends... for so long. But in a way, it was also inevitable.

So Rae and I went our separate ways and I eventually gained perspective, letting her settle into an appropriate place in my history, by and large forgetting. In time her adolescent power, already well past its expiration date, no doubt faded. I knew from one of her sisters that she sold real estate in New Jersey, that she had a son, and in time a second divorce. It all seemed disappointingly ordinary.

Then, because we live in a world where we can do so, I idly googled her a few years back, and shocking stories surfaced. She had been arrested for the attempted murder of her ex-husband, waiting for him in the backseat of his car in the parking lot of his workplace and stabbing him in the neck with a kitchen knife, a week before he was to marry someone else. "In a scene out of a Hollywood shocker," one article read, "he stumbled through the building's doors with blood streaming from his throat..."

One of Rae's friends told reporters she had recently fallen and suffered a concussion and may not have been "quite right" when she did this. He insisted it was not a "jealous wife" thing. The court was apparently not sympathetic. Rae was convicted and sentenced, but about a year later, she died of cancer. My theory is that she was already sick when she stabbed her ex, and that it was a form of cancer that affected her brain. How else can I file this knowledge away with my own memories of Rae?

It's strange to zoom out and see the whole trajectory of a life; it's stranger still to see someone once so close to you transformed into a headline. Was she a mean girl? Sometimes. But Rae was so much more, and so much less. I choose to remember her the way she was that day at the creek beneath the overpass, eating toffee, sharing secrets, singing with me about a time and place that waited for us somewhere, both of us fully believing it did.

Salvation

Gloria Sloane lived on Tamarack Street in a plain-looking house with a chain link fence in front. The door opened to a living room whose drab tobacco-colored carpet was offset by paisley print curtains; there was a shapeless sofa, a blanket-draped armchair, and a rocker in need of repair, all of which were angled toward the television set, a small window of flickering gray light. An unkempt philodendron twisted its tendrils of heart-shaped leaves along sills and shelves and Gloria inhabited the place like a captive watching for the moment to flee. Her mother was a small thin woman from Ireland with a lilting brogue and the disquieting habit of pausing mid-sentence and mid-sweep of broom to ominously acknowledge the presence of beings unseen. Leprechauns hid her slippers and banshees screeched in her ears, but I found her eccentricities endearing.

It was Gloria's father that I feared. He was so volatile and bad tempered I went out of my way to avoid him. He had white hair and watery blue eyes; his belly strained against the undershirt that was his usual attire, and he didn't seem to like anybody, but I was convinced that he hated me special. One day when I showed up to visit, he rose from his chair and demanded that I leave. Then he followed me outside where he lifted my bike from the grass and threw it over the fence onto the street. I have no idea what went on within the family, but just as he had pitched my bicycle over the fence, I could imagine Mr. Sloane flinging plates and kitchen chairs. Maybe Mrs. Sloane's banshees and leprechauns served to lap up some lingering pool of fear and resentment, or perhaps they opened skylights for her, windows to a necessary otherness.

But I would come back again and again, for I loved my friend Gloria, who somehow grew like a rare flower despite all the weirdness. She was fun and imaginative and had a way of making life sound better than it was. When we ventured too far with empty pockets, her heart-rending version of our predicament garnered free pizza. When she started to sneak around with her boyfriend, her x-rated stories were fascinating and instructive, whether or not they were true. And when she recited the poem "Patterns" by Amy Lowell in our school's oratory contest, the audience sat hushed and spellbound. Where she stood on the mundane stage, I pictured garden paths and lime trees, and it was easy to envision her in a pink and silver brocaded gown, her passion laced and stayed but barely contained.

School, meanwhile, was generally just a slow procession of predictables. While teachers dissected the plot of *Silas Marner* or did equations on the board we passed clandestine notes and harvested fuzz balls from our mohair sweaters, learning to sit still and curb the immense push of our nameless desires. Occasionally a brave teacher would organize an ambitious excursion and a busload of students would head out in search of culture at one of the museums or theaters in Manhattan. With this sort of incentive in mind, Gloria and I joined the French Club, accompanying Mrs. Gagnon to an evening performance of *Candide* at the Barbizon Theater. We were dismayed that night to discover that we could not comprehend a single word of French if it wasn't from one of the dialogs we had memorized in the language lab. Still, with Playbills in our hands and perfume in the air, it was possible to imagine living a life someday of intellect and sophistication, even glamour. We watched the blur of lights all the rainy ride home, hoping for more, daring to dream. It was the 1960s, after all, and things were beginning to happen…even on Long Island in a backwater, blue-collar town.

When we are young, we assume the friendships we form will endure forever, but our attention shifts easily and we casually drop what does not in the moment seem relevant. We wish only to travel lightly and have not yet discovered the vast carrying capacity of the human heart. After graduation Gloria and I went to colleges in different parts of the state and vanished quickly to each other. The first semester went by swiftly for me and I was shocked when I learned that Gloria had been doing concurrent time not in college, but a hospital. She had apparently suffered a nervous breakdown, a euphemism whose meaning I did not quite grasp. When I saw her, however, she seemed to have lost her spirit and spark. There was a strange dullness in her eyes and she spoke in a monotone. "I'm still here," she said, "but barely. And I'm not even sure why."

"Well, none of us knows why we're here," I chirped, sounding like a cross between Pollyanna and Sartre, "but in the meantime...well, I don't know...it's interesting...isn't it?"

But the only thing of interest to Gloria was a vision she'd had in the hospital. "I saw a lady standing over my bed holding a white cross made of light," she said. "She gave me hope. I pray to her. I think she'll reappear."

If the lady with the cross had given Gloria a reason to live, it didn't matter to me if she was a figment of imagination, a messenger from God, or the incandescent residue of some powerful antipsychotic medication, but it was as if Gloria were in a holding pattern now, going through motions without enthusiasm, looking beyond the world at hand to some mystifying alternative realm. Her obsession with the vision and her search for what it meant led indirectly to an interest in the literature of the *Watchtower Society*, which provided rules for living, confident answers to existential questions, and prescription for salvation, all of which seemed to satisfy Gloria's deep hunger for some kind of certainty. In time she became a Jehovah's Witness, and from that point on seemed purposeful, engaged, and out of danger.

But I didn't know how to relate to her. Gloria's conversation never seemed to veer far now from the subject of her newfound religion. Because she cared about me, she wanted to convert me, and I listened uncomfortably to her explanations, trying to focus on the good intentions behind them. "Why would you choose to exclude yourself from salvation?" she asked me once. Actually, my inclination would have been to keep all options open, and if I had disqualified myself, it certainly wasn't intentional, but what could I say? I guess I was polite and evasive.

Meanwhile, Mr. Sloane had died of a heart attack, and Gloria was haunted by the fear that his soul was irrevocably lost for all eternity. "I could not bear to go on," she told me, "if it all just ends in nothing." I didn't much like that prospect either, but I couldn't make the leap that Gloria had taken. I felt no virtue or superiority in this. My own religion, if that's what it was, sat shapeless and benign on a back shelf somewhere, and I sort of figured I could tend to it later. I was distressed indeed by the prospect of mortality, which I knew to be true but only in the abstract way youth knows this. Mostly I felt that I was at the very beginning of some grand and wondrous epic, and I didn't want to focus on what happened at the end. I still loved Gloria, but I wanted to laugh with her again, be young with her, live out our hopes and dreams in the real and distracting world.

It wasn't meant to be. Gloria and I were on different paths. She seemed disturbingly firm in all her convictions, and this somehow underscored my own doubt and confusion. Why was I so skeptical? Why would I not even consider the guidelines? The last time I saw her, Gloria looked at me with fondness and pity as though from a very great distance, and it was depressing. She honestly cared about my fate, but I could not be saved.

And so I stepped into the rowdy chaos of life. It wasn't exactly a free for all: there were many rules already in place, plenty of myths had been crafted to illuminate, and conscience had its own robust voice. Within these parameters I would make my share of blunders, laughing and crying and stumbling around, inconsistent and bewildered. I occasionally glimpsed angels and trusted secretly in something hopeful that had taken root in me early on, but I mostly believed in books and bicycles, in the way the sky looked in the mornings, in the triumphs of music and the mysteries of the human heart. I was callow and untrue and I sometimes hurt others but I tried and I loved and I grew. Again and again I saw that many things were simply senseless or unknowable but I submitted to the compelling wonder of now. I began to understand that larger forces shaped me and I was part of an endless cycle that moved me along as powerfully as the tides. I learned to live with ambiguity just as I would learn to live with sorrow and loss, and these things made me human.

From Above

When I was eighteen years old and had never had the experience of flying in an airplane, my boyfriend Richie arranged for us to go on a half-hour cruise above Long Island in a small private Cessna. If I remember correctly, the pilot was not yet fully certified and was trying to accumulate additional flight hours, so this frivolous little expedition was a good excuse for him to practice. We met him at the airport, gave him some money, and climbed on board. I was quite nervous, but for some reason it seemed essential that I finally take wing, and Richie was proud of having facilitated things. We sped along the runway and were suddenly airborne.

We stayed low and local, cruising above the Great South Bay, the sandy strip of Fire Island, the white fringe of surf with endless sea beyond, then veering back towards the land, dark green with trees...*so* green. It was the 1960s, a time of astonishing growth and development in the suburbs of metropolitan New York, but from the air Long Island still seemed rustic. Its tiny highways curved like silver ribbons through large wooded areas, and the new housing developments appeared as islands of orderly objects set among the arboreal expanses.

I had been aware of the Connetquot River, of course, but now I saw how it meandered from the north, flowing leisurely into Nicoll Bay. And I recognized my neighborhood, sometimes known as North Great River. We circled twice above my family's house on Connetquot Avenue. I could see it in perfect dollhouse detail, the peak of its roof, the two tall pine trees at the front entrance, the oak that stood outside my bedroom window, the long concrete walkway I knew was bordered by hydrangea bushes and a mountain laurel shrub with flowers like pink and white parasols.

I wondered if anyone was at home and if they heard the airplane buzzing above them, never suspecting that I was in it looking down upon them like a god. It was odd how everything became a storybook with distance, hard to believe all the drama and sadness that went on in that charming little house. I noticed from my vantage point in the sky that the house sat on the property at a funny angle to the street. "It's *askew*," I thought, as though that explained something.

There is nothing for me to visit there but graves now. Even the house is gone, burned to the ground years ago, even the oak tree outside my bedroom window beneath which I once sat and daydreamed. But when I was eighteen and flying in that little Cessna, I owned the Island in a way I never had. I understood it, saw how its parts all fit together, and how small it was. I saw, too, that it was gorgeous…oh, it was a truly beautiful place! Maybe it was all a matter of perspective, how you looked at things. But I knew that I would leave. I can't explain it, but I definitely knew.

ALONG THE WAY

Young Ones, Take Heart

The year was 1975. I had a weeklong assignment doing clerical work in a dingy office just outside of Syracuse, and I approached it with my usual fatalism. I guess I accepted this as my place in life back then, at least temporarily. There was a space heater at my feet and a radio on the desk playing *Diamonds and Rust*, and it was winter, as it always seemed to be. On this particular day I was wearing a wool turtleneck sweater, and even in the sweater I felt chilly.

Well, as Joan Baez said, we both know what memories can bring—they bring diamonds and rust. But I happened to hear that song today, and the memories came tumbling back to me, unbidden, not beautiful memories, no blue-eyed vagabond smiling out the window of a crummy hotel over Washington Square ("our breath comes out white clouds, mingles and hangs in the air") but a lonely and confused girl with my name filing invoices and answering phones in an obscure office in upstate New York, and perfecting her most trusty survival skill: typing.

Why did I sentence myself to these bleak and tiny routines? I don't fully understand it even now, other than the obvious fact that I was terribly depressed. I liked that song, though, and when it came on the radio I probably turned up the volume a little. Its sadness resonated with me, its nostalgia for something lost and over. Maybe I, too, was nostalgic, but for things that had never happened, and my yearning had turned to resignation. I was living my young life in a state of over-ness.

And yet, here I am...and to quote a wise Buddhist saying that I seem to be repeating to people *ad nauseum* lately, "When you reach the top of the mountain, don't curse the path that brought you there." In my case, it was a circuitous trail with a lot of wrong turns and dead ends into thorny toxic brush, but I survived somehow, and at the age of thirty, I claimed my life as my own and made a new beginning. But the twenty-five-year-old girl in the turtleneck sweater listening to *Diamonds and Rust* didn't know that yet.

Yesterday I had coffee with Ming, a friend and former student of mine in her late twenties. The first time I set eyes on her was at a Halloween party at Vista de las Cruces School in Gaviota. I was a brand new teacher dressed like a witch, with a severe case of laryngitis. She was a tiny girl, about ten years old, dressed as a fairy princess, looking up at me with wide blue eyes, never letting go of her mother's hand. I mentioned that to her yesterday.

"Oh, yes," she said, "I remember it well. You were mute and I was shy, and neither one of us was herself."

Ming is an impressive young woman today, a world traveler and aspiring human rights worker, winner of a dazzling array of fellowships and awards. But she's dealing with the issues and confusions that people in their twenties face, and she seems more vulnerable than confident. She is poised at the threshold of amazing possibilities, but she's still got that bewildering forest to get through...relationships, student debt, meaningful work...that kind of stuff. Each decision point might be crucial.

Obviously my own youth was not a carefree time, but I often tend to think youth is a carefree time for everyone else. You wake up in the morning radiant and good-looking and nothing on you hurts. Your life stretches out before you as a vast potential, so much of it still ahead. You can enjoy yourself. Take some chances. Learn a lot. It'll all work out. But talking to Ming, I remember that being young is a lot more worrisome and complicated than that, even for the fortunate ones who do not drop out of school and exile themselves to grim little offices in cold dreary towns and waste years doing psychodrama with, pardon the term, some asshole guy with issues of his own. It isn't easy being young.

Coincidentally, I spoke to another friend this morning, a woman named Rosemary, who's about ten years older than I am. I love Rosemary's spirit and the affirmative spin she puts on things. I don't even know how the subject of getting older came up in our conversation, but it might have been related to the fact that she is going to her granddaughter's dance recital this Saturday. "I firmly believe that aging has its compensations," she said. I'm beginning to see that she's right.

It's not as though there comes a moment when everything is solved and settled; that never happens. But you get used to the framework of ambiguity, and you learn to see the small good things in front of you.

"Life is so rich," continued Rosemary, "and I'm so much more attentive now. Roses, for example. I don't think I ever fully appreciated roses when I was young. Now, if someone gives me roses, I'm beside myself. I practically inhale them."

Sometimes we are mute and sometimes we're not ourselves, but I tried to tell Ming—and I wish I could sail back into the past and tell that sad young Cynthia—it really does get better. And yet, there's no way I would have believed it.

Featherberry

When I met Steve Featherberry, I was drawn most to his name. It was its own incongruity, a sweet round noun with a flighty modifier. It sounded like a character from Charles Dickens or Roald Dahl; the bearer of such a name could only be interesting. On our first date, Steve wore tight suede pants, a fashion choice that initially embarrassed me, but I convinced myself this might be the garb of a rock star, or maybe something a rodeo rider would wriggle into for his after-hours revelries. Suede pants seemed to reveal a kind of confidence that could be considered attractive, as long as it didn't slide too close to conceit.

I was in the midst of leaving my husband, which I was handling with all the finesse of a doctor doing surgery with a butter knife. It was a little-by-little kind of removal, definitely painful, and this particular cut had landed me in Madison, Wisconsin, where my friend Cyd was living at the time. Cyd helped me find a furnished room in the home of an elderly couple on Breese Terrace whose idea of decor was mostly knick-knacks and Christmas lights. Whenever you opened the front door, a music box clicked on, and *Lara's Theme* from Dr. Zhivago began to play. My room was downstairs in the basement just a short creep past the utility sink and ironing board, but Cyd brought me a little hanging plant of baby's tears to add a bit of green. I looked for a job, borrowed a bike, and pedaled often through the cold dark streets from Breese Terrace to Cyd's house.

Steve was just the sort of distraction I needed. He was a draftsman for a small company in Madison, which wasn't as easy to romanticize as his colorful last name, but he smoked Lucky Strikes, a serious masculine cigarette. He drove around in a little red Comet, and even owned a sailboat, which he intended to take down to Panama City, Florida for reasons never clear to me, but this greatly enhanced his glamour quotient. I simply liked the sound of it.

It was 1973, but Steve was not a part of the hippie-esque campus community. He was a local boy who had lived there all his life, and he was very handsome in what I imagined was a Midwestern way, lean and Nordic, with tiny wire-framed glasses. He didn't say much, which gave me lots of room to fill in the blanks, but it wasn't hard to discern the fact that Steve was tired of Wisconsin, hated his job, and was brimming with dreams and discontent. I loved this about him. It implied that he wasn't anchored, might yet go places, might launch an adventure and take me along.

My own employment history was beginning to read like a rap sheet. My most recent job had been a three-hour stint in the housewares section of Goldblatt's department store in downtown Chicago, tending to fish platters, punchbowls, skillets, and pots. It was hot and stuffy down there in the bowels of Goldblatt's, but I started out optimistically enough, assuming a helpful, friendly stance, straightening stacks of placemats, and conversing with a colleague about cash registers, feather dusters, and how busy the store would be on rainy Saturdays. Call me crazy, but I needed more. Much more. Three hours had never passed so slowly.

So I deserted my post. I tossed my plastic salesgirl badge into the nearest waste bin and headed out to freedom, stopping only at the personnel office to announce my resignation and mutter something about a family emergency. The woman in the office stared a long moment through her thick glasses, then her lips twitched ever so slightly, and suddenly she laughed, a full-blown laugh. "I'm glad you can find so much humor in the misfortunes of other people," I declared indignantly. Thus ended my career at Goldblatt's.

I told Steve this story on our first date, which may have contributed to his impression of me as a very flaky chick, a hunch he was never quite able to shake. It would have been one thing had this been an isolated incident, but you didn't have to be Sherlock Holmes to observe that there'd been a pattern in my life of false starts, short gigs, and a monumental inability to commit to anything. I had quit college, left my husband, hopped around the country on Greyhound buses, and worked as a Kelly Girl, where each job was by definition temporary, a condition that appealed to me greatly.

But if Steve thought my résumé was sketchy, I believe he might have also found it a bit endearing. Being rootless and without function was apparently part of my charm—I was a wild creature that could not be tamed, no nine to five corral contained me, nor could any city claim me. Because I was still young and cute, my irresponsibility could masquerade as spontaneity, and my terror looked something like quirkiness. I had no idea what I was going to do with my life, and I inhabited a kind of limbo realm, still under the illusion that I had all the time in the world. Boyfriends were an easy diversion, and each man I dated was a blank screen onto which I could project a secret slide show of our possible life together, his interests and career the frame within which I envisioned an identity for myself. I imagined meeting Steve in Panama City someday, where we would live on mangoes, moonlight, and mandolin music. I spared myself the mundane details.

It was fun. Steve bought us Boone's Farm Apple Wine and thick wedges of sharp cheddar cheese and we drove in his Comet to Picnic Point where we watched the sun set and talked about his yearnings. I was a good listener, shaping my mouth into every appropriate response, morphing into the perfect lady for him, inventing myself as someone carefree and brave, filled not with the aching desire for safety but wanderlust instead. I was ready to try anything at this point (other than sustained work), prone to quoting poetry and lighting incense, delightfully impulsive and charming, a Holly Golightly misplaced in Wisconsin, but not so elegant or self-sufficient. I was always eager to meet Steve as soon as he got off work. I encouraged him to quit his boring job and follow his heart. We could be free spirits together.

And on Madison nights we met in his waterbed, where every motion rippled and repeated, and afterwards we would hold hands as we floated away into sleep. It was like safely drifting on a great harmless sea. In the morning the alarm would sound and Steve would turn it off and light a Lucky Strike in one fluid motion. I found this incredibly sexy. I would keep the covers over my head, not so much to shield myself from daylight as to shield him from the sight of me with my eye make-up smudged. After smoking his cigarette and drinking black coffee, he would kiss me good-bye and head off to work. Later, I would sometimes ride my bike along the lake and bring back gifts of strawberry jam, or a candle, and once a St. Christopher medal for him to wear on a chain around his neck. Jobs weren't panning out for me but I wasn't trying that hard. Mostly I would busy myself doing nothing. Life is lovely when the entire day belongs to you, even Tuesdays and ten a.m.'s…at least for a while.

Now and then we went for a sail. I wore an embroidered cotton blouse, heavy Levis, and wedge-soled sandals, not a very nautical look, but I topped it all off with a colossal orange life vest and sat stiffly on board, trying to appear at ease. Did I mention that I couldn't swim? There were few things less appealing to me than venturing out in a small craft. But I remained enthusiastic, a good sport even when my nose was sunburned, my jeans damp and stiff, my knuckles white from clutching. I wasn't ready to tell Steve I viewed the deep Wisconsin lakes as gaping liquid tombs.

Mercifully, our outings on the boat were uneventful, the water mostly calm. (I have always preferred monotony to terror.) Only once did a bit of weather roll in, and the boat careened about like a flimsy toy, but Steve seemed to enjoy the challenge, darting about the deck with great confidence, doing whatever sailors do. It may have been his finest moment. As for me, I silently prayed for good ground under my feet, fighting the urge to be sick. I began to see that the boat thing could become an issue.

Apart from the sailing and the weirdness of Breese Terrace, I enjoyed my time in Madison, especially in springtime. Only people who have lived in winter's clutch for six long months can appreciate the euphoria of the first warm days of spring, when suddenly the very earth seems to breathe. Smells returned: saplings, mud, patchouli oil. Shirtless boys threw Frisbees while slender coeds positioned themselves like ladyfingers on the lawns, tanning their milky legs. The white dome of the capitol glinted in the sunlight, the lakes sparkled, and people bicycled happily in the brisk bright air. Girls wore gauzy blouses from India in wonderful rainbow colors and let their long hair frizz and flow. Even the dogs sported bandannas.

But it was becoming increasingly hard to sustain my fantasy about Steve and the life we might share. On some level I realized that I—a fraud and a parasite—had no right to judge him, but I just wasn't getting enough material to work with. He seemed as constant and uncomplicated as a cinder block. He disliked his job but relied on the income, and he wasn't about to cut loose and take a chance. What's more, he began to suggest that I might consider going back to school, or at the very least, find more substantial employment, and maybe make a long-term plan. Good suggestions, all of these, but he was sadly underestimating the extent of my disturbance.

Flight held more appeal than fight, particularly as I wasn't at all sure I liked the way this story was unfolding. I'd loitered in Madison for a good three months trying to be spunky even when nauseous. It was clearly time for me to take a trip. After a last romantic evening and vague promises of return, I boarded a Greyhound and headed to upstate New York...again to an old friend with a sofa. Steve was loath to see me go, but he thought it was downright gutsy and he envied my freedom.

I had never known what beautiful penmanship Steve Featherberry had. His letters were written in blue ink, with large, graceful loops and curls, sometimes illustrated, and all filled with terms of endearment. He awaited my return. He would drive out to retrieve me. He called me his lady and said life was bleak without me. He was ready to leave his job and set sail for Panama City, but not without me.

I was flattered, but distracted, for I had already met someone else—a boozy anthropologist whom I inexplicably found charismatic. He was divorced, ten years my senior, and connected to a world that seemed to hold potential, a path, perhaps, to completeness. Now I was preparing recipes by Julia Child and James Beard for people I didn't even realize were pretentious. I was proclaiming my love for whatever music he played, heading to campus to see films by Bergman and Kurasawa, and reading books about rites of passage in New Guinea and the myth of mental illness. I had even enrolled in school, primarily out of embarrassment. I was reshaping myself for someone else's screen.

"I'm gonna come out there," Steve told me on the phone.

"That isn't good," I said, and tried to explain. "I've *changed*. And don't you think

I needed to? How much longer could I dart from place to place, quitting jobs, hanging around, always depending on the kindness of strangers?"

"But I was never a stranger," Steve protested, not even slightly repulsed by my pathetic attempt to sound like Blanche DuBois as an emerging feminist. "I loved you. I was a better version of myself when you were with me."

It was pointless. I was already gone. Steve's calls stopped and his letters dwindled. A new production played out its course, this one with the alcoholic professor, a waste of several years, but I guess we do what we must do. Eventually I left him too.

There was no man in my life now, and because I had no experience at inventing dreams of my own, I borrowed part of Steve's. I rode a Greyhound for twenty hours and got off in Panama City. I made my way to the beachfront at the Gulf of Mexico, a nameless girl, a backpack and bandanna type with long brown hair who stood on a splintered boardwalk and lifted her scratched sunglasses to better see the view. It was all slow motion and alien silence; the air was humid and smelled like fish. I checked into a motel room at four o'clock in the afternoon, drew the blinds, and sat on the edge of a bed, wondering why I was there. The next morning I got back on the bus and returned to New York to finish school.

I survived all of it: immense loneliness, immense fear, the horror of believing you're nothing. In the decades that passed, I lived many incarnations, most of them best forgotten. And I'm fine now. Grown up, real, and settled down. But sometimes in my sidetracks and impatience, in my fondness for a wander, in the odd sound of my own laugh, and the sense late at night that I am brittle and light and might blow away with the next gust of wind, sometimes I recognize the girl I used to be.

Rising From The Ashes

It's funny how a song can evoke the feeling of a time in such startling detail. Today I heard *The Broadway Hotel* by Al Stewart, and it toppled me abruptly into 1976, like Alice falling into the rabbit hole. There's nothing significant to me about this song at all except the fact that it must have been playing on the radio when I briefly lived in Washington, D.C., if you want to apply any form of the verb *live* to my time there. I haven't written much about the D.C. period of my life, probably because it was bleak and miserable and very short, and I've never been able to find any humor in it.

But when Al Stewart was singing about the *Broadway Hotel* and the *Year of the Cat*, I was working at one of those temporary office jobs where you show up to type or file or complete some task so numbingly boring and mindless you want to scream but you keep your reality to yourself, do the job, and move on. This particular business was somewhere off the Beltway, technically in Maryland, and consisted of two men who told me they were food brokers. I wasn't terribly curious as to what exactly this meant, but there were indeed food products in the office, mostly packaged ham.

I often paired a skirt with a black Danskin leotard for work in those days, just because that's how I used to dress, at least when I wasn't hiding under a big khaki green parka. "Um…we were wondering," said one of the men one day, approaching me with trepidation. "We were wondering if you were a dancer. Or something. Well, when you're not doing this." No, I said, but volunteered nothing more, since I wasn't really sure what I was, whether I was doing this or not. He must have liked me, though. He gave me a canned ham to take home.

Home at the time, if you want to call it home, was an apartment in Bethesda, rented by my then-husband who was really already sort of my ex-husband, but we hadn't yet legalized the divorce and I had returned for temporary shelter after a few months of riding Greyhound buses and hanging around in places like Syracuse. Returning felt a little like suicide to me, but he saw it as our getting back together. Anyway, the apartment building was called the Topaz House, one of those late 1960s structures with a plain beige hotel-like exterior, balconies and elevators, a bank of postal boxes and directory of names. I cannot recall which floor our apartment was on, but if you went all the way to the roof, there was a swimming pool with empty deck chairs lined up here and there, a chlorine smell and a chlorine kind of feeling. My not-quite-ex had gone across the street to "Cort Furniture, Quick Delivery, Easy Rental for Home or Office" and efficiently filled the place with brown and black furnishings, some of them plaid. There was a brand new blank calendar on the white wall of the kitchen area and a poster in the bedroom of a boat in a bay at sunset.

Did I mention that I was depressed? I'm not blaming anybody, either. I just didn't know what I was doing with my life. I was enrolled in a journalism program at American University, and it would have been perfect for me, had I not been emotionally disturbed. I dropped out after three days and took a new job as a hostess…not even a waitress…at a place in Georgetown called *Déjà vu*. I stood around in a black dress and led people to their tables and listened to various lines from men who wondered what I was doing when I wasn't doing this, and just before closing I sometimes drank vodka with the wait staff who were fond of ice cold shots of Stolichnaya. Then I walked across the lonely parking lot at four in the morning and found my way back to the Topaz House.

Even *I* knew this wasn't healthy, nor was it fair to my not-quite-ex, who was really a very nice man. Finally, on a bitter cold January day, I drove nonstop from the parking garage of the Topaz House to my family's home on Long Island, where I went upstairs and slept for forty-eight hours. Yes, there was a family home then, which means my father was still alive, and some siblings still lived there, and it was a place to go if you didn't mind being a painful disappointment to everyone who mattered. Unfortunately, I minded. So I left again and went upstate—upstate New York in winter, great choice for a depressed person. Predictably, things got worse before they got better, but the important thing is, they *did* get better, and even after all these years I'm still surprised, relieved, and grateful.

But let's go back and then fast forward, because there's one moment I want you to witness. I am in another office, back in Syracuse again, but I am beginning to understand that my life belongs to me. I have managed to turn thirty and complete a degree in public administration, whatever that means, and I am doing something professional and serious at this office having to do with buses and social service agencies, things that involve committees and briefings and boring documents, but I know this is not my true calling and I have decided to leave and Go West, and this will be a going without a coming back. The idea is like a flame now, lighting me from inside.

There happens to be a young woman from Canada in the office with me at this time. She's about my age and does clerical work; she's a temp, as I so often was, and she has her own quirky style, and I like her. She is the first one I confide in about my leaving, the leaving that is definitely on the calendar and will take place very soon. I tell her that I will first go to Phoenix, because I have a friend there, and afterwards, who knows? I am leaving for good; that much is certain. By now we have exited the 1970s, thank goodness, but that insipid song about the Broadway Hotel might still be playing on the radio in our little upstairs office, though maybe it's Tom Petty doing *Refugee*...nothing melancholy. I'm practically out of here.

"Phoenix," she says, looking up from the papers and files that mean nothing to either of us. "Will you rise from the ashes?" Then she reaches around to the back of her neck and unclasps a necklace I have admired that belonged to her grandmother. It's yellow, like sunshine and saffron and light. It's *yellow*.

"Take it," she says.

Sometimes it is the stranger who sees who you really are. Yes, I know I would have gotten through without that special totem, but I felt fortified, somehow, and understood. Maybe that's all you need. And I wore the yellow necklace across the continent, and I wore it across decades, and I have risen from ashes more than once.

She's Your Mother

I wrapped myself in plastic, donned gloves and a surgical mask, and sprayed myself with insect repellent. I was about to enter the house on Long Island for the first time in twenty years. Set back from the road at the end of a long walkway bordered by blue hydrangeas, its brick face and blistered paint looked familiar and sad. Flea-bitten cats wandered about the yard and meowed morosely from within. Rubbish spilled from boxes and plastic bags by the doorway, and a desolate shopping cart brimmed with cans and shoes, planks of wood and wet newspaper, an old wool hat and a hubcap. Long ago my father watched for me through those windows now broken and boarded, and kept the yellow porch light on until I arrived. There was no one to greet me now.

My mother, who had just been hospitalized, had been living alone in this house for many years, filling it and filling it, to drive away the emptiness, I guess. Still, I was not prepared for the shock of what awaited me when I pushed open the front door. From ceiling to floor were boxes and stacks of newspapers, mail, magazines, and clothing, many draped with sheets or adorned like shrines with small toys, knick-knacks, tools... all manner of random objects. It was simply a vast emporium of stuff, dusty and filthy, with a narrow trail through which to walk. Fourteen cats inhabited the place, skinny and nearly feral, flies buzzed around paper plates of cat food, and one cat suddenly leapt down from a stack of boxes, scaring a scream out of me.

"So what happened?" asked George, a congenial Greek who had been my mother's neighbor since 1983. "You go away and forget your poor mother? You forget to come back?"

How could George understand that all of my mother's children were exiles? We had not felt welcome here since my father's death in 1978. By this time we were living in four different states—the nearest son was a twelve-hour drive away, and I had flown in from the other coast.

Even as children, we knew that our mother had her issues, and the hoarding problem was a dominant theme. She became frantic when we tried to clean and throw things out or explore the mysteries of closets, drawers and stashes. She referred to that kind of exploration as "rummaging", and it was a delicious crime punishable by screaming tirades that would last for hours, but it was sometimes worth the risk. After all, our own belongings were often confiscated—a new toy we never got to play with, a bracelet whose colored stones I admired briefly on my wrist, dresses with the tags still on confined to a barricaded closet and saved for some vague tomorrow that never came. In an act of rebellion shortly before I moved to California, I kidnapped three dolls from the attic closet in which they had been held: two that had belonged to my two sisters, which I returned to each of them, and my own porcelain bride. My mother's wrath was monumental. I had committed an unforgivable transgression of which she bitterly spoke for years thereafter.

We all moved on.

"Oh, I've seen worse," said Eileen, the social worker from Adult Protective Services, who had come to meet me and was checking out the yard. "And they always have cats. Half my damn job is getting rid of cats." I had already called upon the services of a volunteer worker from the SPCA to help gather up the animals, a small blonde woman named Dottie who arrived with a sack of cat food and a cardboard box. She expertly cased the area, opening windows and coaxing the cats with the smell of the food. They came to her and rubbed against her legs, and she gently held them in her hands and promised to find them good homes. I could not fathom how anyone would take this on.

Indeed, my world was suddenly peopled with a ragtag network of eccentric strangers upon whose kindness I depended completely. They were inexplicable to me, spontaneously appearing to help trap cats and guide me through the erratic recesses of my mother's life. "Oh, there's Selena!" shouted Linda, the next-door neighbor. "She's your mother's favorite." I had actually heard of Selena—she was the cat my mother once told me had a human face, the cat that looked at her with absolute understanding, as nobody else ever did. Dottie promised to adopt Selena herself.

Meanwhile, a sanitation guy named Frank had come over to help assess our clean-up needs. He wandered about, pursing his lips, looking as intently as a physician about to offer a diagnosis. "She must have missed your father terribly," he said, offering to provide two dumpsters for the price of one, and for an extra two hundred, a couple of laborers too. I told him that I'd ask my brothers, who would be arriving soon to clear out the house, retrieve some belongings, and list the place with a realtor. "They don't know what they're in for," said Frank.

"We tried to help," said Linda. "She was coming over forty times a day for coffee. And she would go out walking at all hours. Sometimes she'd call my husband from a phone booth at one in the morning, asking to be picked up from East Islip or someplace. We all figured the family had reasons for staying away."

There were reasons, yes. But standing there amidst the sorrowful debris of an old lady's life, I was unable to explain or justify. "There's a lot of pain here," I submitted lamely.

"Pain? Who doesn't know pain?" said George. "Look at me. My mother, my wife, my new girl...all of them gone. Just like that. But I'm strong. You must be strong, young lady!" He pointed me towards his own ramshackle house, diagonally behind my mother's yard. "Now go in bathroom. Fix hair. Put on the make-up. Be strong."

At four o'clock I went to the hospital, where my mother had been placed in a psychiatric unit. I carried a laminated card with her room number, and I pressed a special buzzer on the elevator to gain admittance. The nurse brusquely inspected the shopping bag I bore, pulling out sweatpants, slippers, a new shirt, a hairbrush; everything was deemed acceptable. I wondered fleetingly if she was looking at me with pity or disdain. Was I the daughter of that loony lady? Or the selfish one who abandoned her poor mother? Nothing registered but complete indifference. She pointed to the room.

My mother sat in bed, her yellowing white hair in a ponytail, and looked at me calmly. She had been given anti-depressants and anti-psychotics, and seemed to be enjoying a reprieve from her depression and obsessions. I asked her why she hadn't called to let me know she needed help. "I was ashamed," she said. "All of a sudden, it hit me. I don't know how it got so bad, but it was out of control. And I was so depressed. I kept looking back, dwelling on the past, missing the old days. I didn't have any desire to do anything."

A round-the-clock nurse had been posted at her bedside because she was considered an elopement risk, but it was clear to me that my mother had no inclination to go anywhere at the moment. "I needed a rest," she said, and over and over, she asked about her cats. She seemed to be under the impression that the house required a little tidying up but that afterwards she would return. Amazingly, she began to reveal secrets of her kingdom—there was cash under a certain cushion, a gold locket in a closet, letters and photos in a chest of drawers upstairs, legal documents in a steel file cabinet completely buried under coats and newspapers in the front room. She was telling me to rummage, take things. I dreaded reentry, but I realized was necessary to assess and salvage.

It was eerie to be alone inside the house. I gingerly stepped through the debris, trying to make sure no animals were trapped inside as I squeamishly poked around for any recognizable treasures in the piles. There were notes to my beloved dead brother still taped on the refrigerator, and words written in charcoal on the walls. There was a peanut butter jar that appeared to be filled with pee, and unwashed tins of cat food, and Plaid Stamps from 1959, books of them, never redeemed. Packages I mailed to my mother lay unopened on the floor, addressed in my own handwriting. There were framed images of my siblings and me, and my father's diplomas, and an oil painting he never finished. There was the oval mirror in front of which my sisters posed when one became a bride, and a black-bordered magazine picture of Bobby Kennedy that I'd torn from a magazine in 1968 and taped to the wall near my bedroom, and a stack of my brother's old comic books, and the vintage train case I once took to slumber parties on summer nights.

This was my family house, and it would at last yield its mysteries and troves of goods. I could rummage freely...but I no longer cared. Everyone was gone, everything was silent, and all I felt was the pain of lost childhood, my father's absence, a tragic sense of waste. I was suddenly a little girl again, and I didn't know what to do about my mother, about this house, about anything.

Then I noticed the butterfly tray atop a dresser in the attic, illuminated like a stained glass window by a shaft of dusty sunlight. Someone had already broken into the house and taken the television and conspicuous valuables, but this beautiful object had been overlooked. An arrangement of butterfly wings under glass that my father had brought back from South America long ago, its iridescent blues and luminous yellows had fascinated me when I was a child. Now it seemed like a link to something good from the past. It's what I chose to keep.

The hospital was eager to release my mother, but all agreed that she could not go back to the house and was clearly incapable of living alone. I drove around the bleak streets looking at adult homes willing to accept a woman whose sole income was Social Security. I was referred to a legal aid attorney. "You're looking at the bottom of the barrel," he said.

My brothers began to advocate that we relocate our mother to a facility in California, since two of her children lived there, including me. They pointed out the unlikelihood of our visiting if she were left in New York, and were also convinced that if she were placed within fifty miles of the house, she would probably try to return to it. My sister managed to discover a relatively pleasant assisted living residence in Orange County that agreed to take her, and unbelievably, I found myself shopping for the best deal on a one-way ticket.

"I am bringing her here," I kept thinking, and I was filled with fear. I became a client, an advocate, a nervous wreck, a stranger in my own life. I spent hours in the Social Security office, was guided through paperwork, received advice and instructions from counselors, social workers, bureaucrats, and friends.

"She was an awful mother," I confided to a lady named Edna, a volunteer at the Area Agency on Aging. "She ruined our childhoods. This isn't even someone I actually love."

"This isn't about love, dearie," replied Edna without sympathy. "It's about moral duty and human decency. She's your mother."

And so she is, and thus began my East Coast mother's unexpected California life. After months of tears and medication her memories dimmed, and the trauma of upheaval and loss gave way to passivity and acceptance, and the years have fled. I have remained her steadfast visitor, doing my best to tend to her needs as her frailty and dementia take their toll. It's a depressing and wearisome duty, I admit it...and it's gone on *so* long. And yet, in a weird, paradoxical way it sometimes feels rewarding too; in this last part of her life, my mother has inadvertently taught me how kindness, duty, and forgiveness cleanse the soul.

She was always overwhelmed—I can see that clearly now. With six kids and a turbulent marriage that her strict Jewish parents had vehemently opposed, no real social or support networks, and an uncontrollable propensity for anxiety and hysteria, *of course* she felt beleaguered. I even think she did the best she could. But some memories are better blurred, and my mother's inability to recall all the strife and sorrow is probably a merciful forgetting.

Her countenance these days is relatively cheerful; people at the facility know her only as an endearingly eccentric old lady, and they look out for her, giving her a hand when she seems especially bewildered. A few months ago she took a terrible fall outside, broke her hip and cracked her head on a concrete step, and she somehow got through it, painfully but with a humbling kind of resilience. For her ninetieth birthday, we held a little celebration with cake and balloons, the first birthday party she ever had in her whole life. She continues to collect—even in her room, the drawers are curiously crammed, her closet crowded to capacity, and every space filled. Some treasures are wrapped in napkins.

I too hold onto things. Perhaps it is natural for ephemeral beings to accumulate stuff, to seek comfort and solidity in objects. For me, these tend to be items whose chief value is in the memories with which they are associated, and I delude myself with the idea that holding onto such artifacts enables me to keep a vestige of what has irrevocably vanished. Letters and documents are the worst of this tyranny; I have a large trunk in the garage filled with papers that can bring me to my knees with sadness. (It's been suggested that I burn them, but they have become somehow sacred, and even if I don't want to read them, I'm not ready to destroy what truths they may contain.)

In the case of my mother, who grew up in poverty and never felt secure, maybe sovereignty over a vast realm of possessions meant having finally arrived. Or maybe the voices inside her head did not echo so loudly in a house muffled with stuff. Or maybe, and most likely, it's all just obsessive compulsion, no back story needed.

She's my mother. I have come to accept the strange permutations of loneliness, and to view with compassion the havoc wrought by brain chemistries gone awry. I know there are reasons for what families do and fail to do, and that what seems like indifference is often simply pain. I have learned to retrieve from the rush of time that which is worthwhile, and to release that which can only cause anger or sorrow. But I also understand that sometimes it is necessary to look back and look hard before leaving for good.

My Italians

First I must learn the art of waiting. It's what we seem to do here in this Neapolitan town. We walk, and we wait. We congregate, and we wait. There is always someone missing whose presence is essential, some preordained time that has not yet arrived, some inexplicable sequence of events that must unfold. The waiting is an integral part of the experience of being here, and because I do not speak the language and cannot fill it with words or grab hold of the ones in the air around me, I am learning to sit still and observe. I am learning to be less intimidated by idleness and uncertainty, learning to relinquish a bit of control.

In fact, I began writing this in a notebook while sitting on a bench with my uncle, Zio Pinuccio, at the edge of a municipal garden by the River Sarno in Scafati. He told me (I think) that this river was once an important navigation route to the sea, which made this area the site of one of the earliest settlements in Italy. In the old days, I think he said, the river was beautiful, and people came to fish from its banks, but now it is polluted because of factories upstream. In our stroll around the park, my uncle and I have contemplated an enormous palm tree whose huge trunk is riddled with bullet holes, enjoyed the shade of tall pines and the pinks and pale purples of hydrangea in bloom, and witnessed a peacock presenting an astonishing display of feathers to an indifferent hen. Now teenagers loiter noisily by a fountain, a young couple is kissing on a secluded bench, and an old man pedals by on a bicycle. In short, there is nothing and everything happening, and we are sitting here to wait (I think) for Luca.

I don't mind, really. It's nice to sit in silence next to someone you like. I only wish I had brought along a book and a bottle of water. A few minutes ago I ventured to ask (no doubt in very distorted Italian) if there might be a place nearby where I could buy something for the two of us to drink, but the meaning of this question and its profound importance to me has somehow eluded my uncle, for he brushes it off with a phrase that ends in *dopo*...later....and we remain true to our single purpose, which apparently is to sit here waiting. At one point I invite him to listen to some music on my iPod, and at the sound of Bach's *Goldberg Variations*, he smiles, tilts his head back, closes his eyes and lets the pleasure of the music transport him. It becomes a moment I will never forget, and the *Goldberg Variations* will forever bring me back to it.

Zio Pinuccio's father and my grandfather were brothers, and because he is thus a first cousin to my own father, I feel a special bond with him, and in his eyes I see something familiar and dear. His eldest son, Gianni, who speaks English, tells me this about Zio Pinuccio: "He suffers because he is an idealist about the world and he is disappointed. He thought the world would change but it did not."

And yet, there is no one more filled with wonder and appreciation than my uncle for beauty and art and the nobler gestures of humanity. We walk in the coolness of the church of *Santa Maria Vergini* and he points to the graceful curves of marble decoration, the paintings on the domed ceiling, the way the light enters through an arched window. We wander slowly among the ruins of Herculaneum with his wife, my Zia Titina, noticing the detail of a border on a wall, the precisely wrought image of a bird, the warm Pompeian reds. He navigates through the congested streets in his little green car, his hair an unruly cloud of white curls, and he points to Mt. Vesuvius, and even if I could speak perfect Italian, I would not be able to find the words to tell him how much he means to me.

Here in Italy I must learn to let go of the English that moors me, and splash around in Italian. "It's a difficult language," admits Gianni. "So many tenses, so many nuances. English for me is crisp and clean, like programming a computer, but Italian is good for diplomacy. It leaves the listener more room for interpretation."

So I walk around starry-eyed and confused, carrying my trusty *dizionario* and a book of verb conjugations everywhere I go, periodically retreating into my notebook to painstakingly formulate my own awkward sentences, then reciting them like a child to an indulgent audience. I listen for the occasional shine of meaning in the river of talk around me, and the sounds and rhythms of Italian begin to fill my very dreams. I see now what immersion really means, and I feel lost and helpless, at times shutting down with the exhaustion of trying to maintain meaningful engagement. I will not be here long enough to even begin to attain competence, but sometimes communication happens. Sometimes the words come. Sometimes they are not needed.

I learn, too, to ignore the clock and say yes to new experiences and adventures. If you are offered a plate of chewy *sconcigli* or *il piede e il muso* (which may well give you pause), try it. If it's nearly eleven on a Monday night and you are mentally ready for bed and Nello proclaims this a good time to see Napoli by night, the best response is *andiamo*. Espresso at midnight? You can sleep when you're dead. A ride with Luisa on the back of her motorcycle to an early morning market where you will taste an icy *granita* for the first time and later wait for her while she buys a whole octopus for dinner? *Sì.* Invitations to meet distant relatives, friends of distant relatives, friends of friends of distant relatives? *Meraviglioso!* Hot, sweaty, bitten by mosquitoes? Deal with it.

It's a tricky zone we must traverse to enter something different, and it changes us. A spirit of openness and responsiveness begins to take hold of me, a spirit that I hope will carry over into my ordinary everyday life. I have walked to a waterfall in the mountains above the Amalfi Coast with my cousin Luca and Maestro Vincenzo, heard Zio Mario sing an old street vendor song about *zuppa di polpo*, and drunk of the healing waters of the fountain at Castellammare di Stabia. I have been kissed and showered with affection enough to last a lifetime. I will never be the same.

Which brings me to the most important thing I have learned from my Italians, which is to gracefully accept when love is given. My grandfather left Italy in 1905. Period. I have no other link to this place. When I showed up here eighty years later, these people might have easily and understandably dismissed me as a stranger. Instead, they took me into their hearts and have welcomed me whenever I have returned in the course of three decades. No small gift, this. No small miracle.

I look back now, remembering the narrow Neapolitan streets, laundry hanging from the windows, lovers on benches by the sea, late-night gatherings at tables covered with floral-printed cloths. I recall the fireworks of each nightly *festa*, the familiar profile of Vesuvius through summer haze, laughter and arguments in that beautiful and elusive language. And I think about this unequivocal and irrational love I have inherited, and none of it is lost in translation. This is the family with whom I have had no pain, other than the sadness of saying good-bye to them each time I leave. I suppose one could write it all off as a fantasy, but again and again it's been reaffirmed. They are my kind and generous *famiglia*. They saw fit to perceive me as real and receive me as their own. I finally understand, and I accept.

A Card From Nova Scotia

A postcard arrived from my old friend Helen—she was thinking of me in Nova Scotia. The card had a photo of a red and white lighthouse on an outcropping of granite boulders, a place scoured by waves and weather, ruggedly picturesque, clean and faraway. I always liked the idea of Nova Scotia, even if it's just the chance to say its satisfying name. *Nova Scotia*, I whispered. I like the way it almost rhymes and goes from scratch to softness and lets your lips twice form a circle. I stood by the mailbox imagining Helen there.

But Helen-in-Nova-Scotia just set me to thinking about the Helen I knew in another time and place: Oneonta in the fall of 1970, when the two of us were college girls together. In rustic contrast to the Long Island suburbia from which we'd come, upstate New York was woods and cows and narrow country roads. Its loveliness tugged us from our classrooms, for we were easily distracted and willingly enchanted by anything but school. Helen dressed like a co-ed from a catalog then, in sweaters and skirts and brown leather boots, her blonde curls escaping from beneath a knit hat. We often cut classes just to walk among the yellow leaves and smell the air with its hints of smoke, its banquet of decay.

Were we missing our boyfriends, or did we already know how little we cared? Were we yearning to travel, or were we fully immersed in the brilliance of the glinting day? Once we came upon an old abandoned house and audaciously entered rooms still piled helter-skelter with broken furniture and small stacks of letters that spoke of grief and rapture, reviling base humanity and alleluia praising God. It was a house of mystery and pain and we a pair of callow voyeurs, rifling through the ruins of someone else's life, while our own lives waited shapeless and blank to begin.

What did we know? We knew nothing. We received strokes of broad-brush impressions; we were drawn like insects to color and light. We touched upon learning, sucked at its sweetness, and darted away to someplace else. We were new and fat with the luxury of endless time, we were glib and untried and answerable to no one really. But we took ourselves seriously. We even thought we suffered, though mostly we loved the words. We bathed in the sentiment of Kahlil Gibran and listened to James Taylor and Leonard Cohen on record players in the dorms. We read Robinson Jeffers and understood divinely superfluous beauty and T.S. Eliot whimpering, wondering yet if we dared to eat a peach, and ee cummings—oh, so of the order of things free so clean punctuation dropped like spare parts. We thought we were uncommon.

We poked about like tourists observing many things through our presumption of superiority. Inside the town, the ladies went by abbreviated names like Bev and Midge, good names for gray pigeons, bobbed hair no nonsense names, names for here and now. They kept clean houses, those ladies did, and gathered in craft circles for paint-on embroidery and holiday decoration. Outside their steamy windows trees were lavishly dropping gold leaves that for a moment floated in the air like music, then fell silently to the street. There was a mail order Sears on Main Street and a tired-looking grocery store, and a couple of shops that catered to the college girls, the kind of places that sold candles and sandalwood incense.

Helen and I had been high school classmates who went our separate ways following graduation, but after two years of commuter schools and Long Island office jobs, we both enrolled at Oneonta, unbeknownst to one another. It was a teacher's college built on a hill, a pretty place filled with earnest young women who made welcome signs for their dorm room doors and were far more likely to be knitting scarves in their rooms than smoking pot, quite a change from Stony Brook, where I'd been before. I shared a room in Littell Hall with a girl named Ruth who tossed all night and wrote bad poetry. I learned how to run a filmstrip projector, a requirement for future teachers, and got A's on papers for classes I seldom attended. I brushed my hair a hundred strokes each night, did sit-ups obsessively, and let my fingernails grow long for the first time in my life so I could paint them frosted pink. I realized this was the wrong school for me and arranged to transfer out as soon as the semester ended, but I was very excited when I saw Helen walking to class one morning.

Helen lived off-campus and had a car, not just any car, but a tiny Triumph convertible, a car like a toy, with a bicycle horn and bucket seats. It was not the car for an upstate winter, but it was delightful for drives on brisk sunny days, and together we had many. Maybe driving around was our therapy. We always indulged in intense conversation as the world slipped by in colored blurs. Then one day when I wasn't there, Helen drove straight into a telephone pole, totaling the Triumph but emerging with only a bump on her head. I went to the infirmary to see her, and I asked her how it happened. "I did it on purpose," she said. "I think I wanted to die, but I only wrecked the car."

How could I have been so oblivious? I knew Helen was unhappy—weren't we all?—but I hadn't seen the self-destructive impulse. It was scary, and Helen seemed numb after that, and instead of driving around, we watched *Days of Our Lives* and *Star Trek* in the dormitory lounge, and pretty soon her boyfriend came back and they got married and he took her to Las Vegas, where he was studying hotel management. I didn't stick around either. A few months later I moved to Chicago to marry *my* boyfriend, who was a medical student there. Many letters were exchanged between Chicago and Las Vegas, and they were all about how trapped we felt. Inevitably, we both left our husbands, nice Catholic boys who'd gotten caught in the confusion, and we each returned to Long Island for temporary refuge, hoping to figure out the next step.

Helen was skinny and stylish now and wore silk blouses in colors like apricot and cream. She smoked cigarettes, drank scotch on the rocks, and had acquired a Ford Granada. We resumed our old habit of aimlessly driving, mostly on Long Island, speeding along Guinea Hills, meandering through a place called Little Africa by the Nesoquogue River, north to the Long Island Sound where the beaches were pebbled and the water lapped upon the shore like a lullaby, out east beyond the potato fields and to the light house at Montauk Point. One day we drove west and north all the way to Oneonta, six pointless hours, then turned around and came back. What were we looking for? I don't have a clue, but it wasn't on Long Island or in upstate New York.

In time we each went further west, as restless souls eventually do. Helen worked for a while in Los Angeles, then married a man older than her father and moved to a condo in Scottsdale. I went to visit them once, and I couldn't understand the attraction. He was retired from a career in insurance, a pot-bellied man with thin white legs, no sense of humor and a great many ailments. They were sitting by the swimming pool listening to Henry Mancini. Helen offered me scotch and salted nuts. She seemed to have suddenly turned seventy.

After that marriage, Helen became unreal to me, and for several years I lost track of her. Eventually she found a good husband who genuinely loved her. Along with him came a house in Pennsylvania, a couple of stepchildren, and religion—the born-again kind, with its enviable certainty. My friend Helen was happy at last.

And then came cancer, because just when things are finally going great, isn't that when the other shoe drops? She told me about it in an email. Mastectomy. Radiation. For a while it was gone, and then suddenly it reappeared and was *in her system*, as she put it. *I am not desperate to fill every single day that is left*, she wrote, *but there is unquestionably the knowledge that each day is a precious gift, and it's time to get on with living and doing. I do believe I still have work to do for the Lord, and when it's time, God will show me what that is. But first, a vacation. I always wanted to go to Nova Scotia...*

Helen thought about me in Nova Scotia, and I am holding her postcard and thinking of her here. Once we knew only beginnings, but lately we can see how stories end. We can see the courage of an ordinary life, the hope in small gestures, how we clean and craft and embroider what is stark, how we clutter, how we cling. And I wonder...who will walk through the ruins of my house? What words will they find? What deeds will have mattered?

Church

Ladies with powdered cheeks and lined lips smiled and greeted us as we entered, and a white-haired gent handed us a bulletin, and we took our seats in a bright airy sanctuary where all the proceedings at the front were projected on a large video screen above the altar. There were many welcomes and handshakes, and children in turquoise robes made a joyful noise as they entered singing and waving palm fronds. A pastor with the demeanor of a neighborly insurance salesman talked of God's love in a broken world, and I hoped to hear one of the old traditional hymns I remembered from childhood, but the choir sang contemporary Christian music. I never would have even been in here but I was visiting my friend Helen in Florida and it happened to be Palm Sunday, and this was important to her.

"That was what they call a blended service," she explained afterwards, somewhat apologetically.

For a moment I thought she said a "blander service", which it certainly was, but I was glad I went; it cured me of the misguided notion that I might really find some greater connection to God in such a context. For many years I drove to churches on Sunday mornings, and I would sit in the back and at the edges, trying to be inconspicuous, testing the waters, seeking a house of worship where I felt I belonged. Now I remembered why I stopped.

I've known other kinds of churches. I think of a certain sandstone cave from which I can see the sea and the contours of the hills, upon whose walls are still visible the fading red spirals and sunbursts painted by those who came here long ago and where the windblown sand that covers the ground is as cool and soft as talcum powder. I think of the time I stood with friends beneath the sycamores when the sparkling percussive music of the universe encircled us—the sound of rain on leaves. It was a sound of whispers and rustling, rising to applause, a sound of tambourines and laughter, a sound that quenched a thirst we didn't know we had. It was sudden and secret and it quickly passed, but we knew we had been blessed.

But back to Florida, which is where I had gone to visit my friend Helen who asked me to accompany her to this particular church, with its affirmative handshakes and instructive readings and contemporary Christian music. Back to Florida, where the moment I stepped outside from the airport in the middle of the night, the humid air covered me with slapdash kisses and the warm breeze brought back a rush of unwelcome memories. Back to Florida, where a group of men with skin like polished ebony stood at the curb by their taxicabs laughing and talking in musical island accents, and one of them drove me to my hotel and I slipped into the room where Helen was asleep and I lay in the dark remembering other times when I was here, usually to visit my sister in Palm Bay, and finally to be at her memorial.

Helen and I have known each other for more than forty years. We were in junior high when we first met, and to be honest, we didn't even like each other back then. We met again in college, and that's when our friendship began in earnest, and there were many twists and turns thereafter, including long stretches when we lost touch, but by chance or intent, we always reconnected. There are friends who walk together for a part of the journey, but others who bear witness to the overall trajectories of one another's lives. With us, it's been the latter.

After the Palm Sunday church service, we go back to the hotel to laze around on poolside chairs, but our best conversation happens unexpectedly, in the middle of the night. I hate that it is precipitated by Helen's waking up in pain, but it's the tumor at the base of her spine. She doesn't like to take the medication unless she really needs it, but by the time she really needs it, the pain has gotten fully entrenched.

I switch on the nightstand lamp between our beds, and a small circle of light envelops us. "I hate to see you suffering like this," I tell her.

"Suffering? This isn't suffering," she says.

During one of the long periods during which we were far apart and seldom in contact, Helen worked in a hospice house. She saw people writhing in agony that drugs could not assuage, crawled next to them in bed and held them. Her own pain, she says, is manageable, and the medication is kicking in, and her face relaxes, and she begins to unfold like a blossom in the pool of warm light. She has already borne this cancer for a decade beyond what doctors allotted her. She tells people it's a God thing.

And in the Florida room in these hours before dawn we sit up in our beds eating almonds and cheese and slices of pear. We talk about how much we love the thrift stores down here where those fancy ladies who have moved from New York deposit their designer castoffs, though maybe not so much now, with the economy as it is. And we talk about the things that need fixing and the values that are slipping and how hard our fathers worked. We talk about what we believe, and what life has taught us. We remember who we were, grateful for the better selves we hope we have become.

I'm still in the fight, Helen likes to say. The cancer is a challenge that has altered everything for her, but she's somehow risen to it, and she tries to do good works, for she still believes she must. But at the same time, is it not gracious to accept ease when it is offered? Are we paying attention? Have we learned from our mistakes? Did we ever imagine it would all go by so fast? The thread of this conversation began to unspool forty years ago. Helen and I pick it up every now and then and continue it with the same fervor we always had. It's a wondrous thing, really, how we update, and question, and confirm.

Dawn nears, and we're sleepy, and a tropical breeze is ruffling the blinds and the decades of our lives, and our beds are small white boats in a Florida room lit with lamplight and blessings.

AT THIS POINT

Not Quite A Crone

Dorothy says my problem is that I am not yet a crone. I am no longer young, this is true, but I have quite a way to go before I attain true crone status. Crone is an ugly word and I am not at all sure I want to become one, but Dorothy explains that it pertains to a woman for whom age has brought wisdom, perspective, and even a certain kind of freedom. Since she is a crone and I am not, Dorothy lovingly offers to be my guide. "It will be like having an older sister," she tells me.

Dorothy is in fact nearly ten years older than I am, but she manages to be beautiful. Her hair is gray, cut very short, and styled in a natural way that frames her elegant features. She is slender and moves like a dancer, and she always dresses well. Dorothy is not afraid to spend money on a good quality purse or a well-cut jacket, and I respect that about her. She is the kind of person who inspires an adjective all her own: *Dorothy-esque*, which can refer to a colorful woven shawl, a finely wrought poem, an honest and probing conversation.

Such conversations are in fact her forte. She was a teacher, counselor, and wellness coordinator at the school where we both worked. Now she leads writing workshops and women's groups in which intimacies are shared, realizations unearthed, emotions expressed, and poems written right there, on the spot. I know all this because I went to one of these Dorothy-esque gatherings once. Participants sat outside in an area shaded by evergreen trees, which gave it a kind of summer camp feeling. Prayer flags fluttered in the breeze, the mountains were visible in the distance, and everyone was welcoming and kind, but it was not my cup of tea. I am a bit skittish and feral, you see. You can gradually lure me in towards the hearth if you're patient, and I may even take my place in the circle, albeit briefly and awkwardly, but then, inevitably, I feel the need to bolt, and I bolt. But Dorothy knows this about me, and she accepts it, and while I consistently decline her invitations to partake of the women's group, she consistently gives me her friendship, one-on-one, instead.

On this particular visit, we walk across Highway 154 and stroll into the heart of Los Olivos, where we encounter a handful of our former students, and it's a little like being famous, which comes with having been a teacher for a long time in a tiny town. A couple of years after they leave you, the kids turn into astonishing young adults who have long ago forgotten the pain of all those essays you made them write, and they look at you in a softer focus, seeing you as the benign, well-meaning advocate you were, and they greet you with affection. As for me, I feel inexplicably proud of them, although I know I played only a miniscule role in their development. At least I did no harm, is what I tell Dorothy. "Oh, we did much better than no harm," she says. "We *inspired* them." I wish I had Dorothy's confidence. Maybe that will come with crone-hood.

We wander over to St. Mark's and Dorothy asks me if I've ever walked the labyrinth. Somehow I didn't even know there was one, so of course we go over there and walk it. It's pretty simple to navigate, not a maze, just a non-branching path to the center, but there's something soothing and meditative about following it, over and over, until at some point I begin to feel dizzy, but in a good way, if that makes any sense.

Dizzy is what I often am lately, or maybe ditzy is a more precise word, a manifestation of my chronic befuddlement. Here's the thing: I have lost my confidence. Lost my edge, if indeed I ever had one. I honestly don't know what I am doing, other than living each day and hoping I am not missing the point. Sometimes I forget how to be with people. Does that sound weird? I become painfully shy and at a loss for words and…well, when

I get this way it's just so much easier not to go out into the world, and yes, I realize I am incredibly blessed that I don't regularly need to. But *shouldn't* I be going someplace? Am I just walking a circular labyrinth?

We go back to Dorothy's house and sit in the backyard and I can hear the music of a fountain as I tell her, half jokingly, that I am thinking of writing a field guide for the befuddled. She reads me a few of the poems she has been working on. As we sit there in the sunlight, the plates in the earth's interior are moving, and pressure is accumulating, and a fault line is about to rupture in Haiti, ten miles from Port Au Prince, and only 6.2 miles underground. The fountain murmurs, a red tail hawk soars in the blue sky above us, and Dorothy's poems are filled with images of light and transformation. Some 3,000 miles from where we sit, unimaginable misery and destruction have been unleashed, but for us, it is a flawless afternoon.

I hear about the earthquake on the radio as I am driving home, and all of the things I fret about seem suddenly silly and self-indulgent, as indeed they are. But the epic and mundane inhabit the same moment, and agony and pleasure are concurrent, and this has always been true, except that now we are relentlessly informed. What do we do with the knowledge? How do we contain this constant barrage of input and all its painful contradictions? There is no way to make sense of things. We live our lives and try to be good people and hope whatever virtue we manifest outweighs any inadvertent harm. We walk our labyrinths, watch the sky, teach and smile at the kids in town. We patch up and hold on, says Dorothy:

> *trusting friendship*
> *and some ruby words like love*
> *hope*
> *gratitude*

And when I'm finally a crone I may do better.

Maps

Some people keep love letters. I have maps—beautifully detailed hand-drawn maps made for me by my husband over the years whenever I was about to set out on a solo adventure or one with my girlfriends, either bicycling, hiking, or driving. It was an era before cell phones, Google earth, and GPS, and my sense of direction has always been notoriously bad, so before I left, Monte would equip me with his meticulous drawings and instructions written in a way that even I could understand. These maps went with me on many trips, and I referred to them often. It was one of the ways he took care of me in those days, and I've never had the heart to throw them away.

I recently came upon the maps in a file box in the garage, where the years have left them faded, yellowed, and soft as tissue paper. Torn and taped and folded many times, most of them outline dirt road loops, trails, and mountain climbs, and many provide a fascinating at-a-glance view of Orange County's (and northern San Diego's) open space and unincorporated backcountry and the preferable ways to access it as it was in the early 1980s. Memorable landmarks are included to help me get oriented, grades and riding surfaces are noted, and potentially confusing choices are explained. I can read "I love you" in every painstakingly drawn squiggle and curve.

It's amazing, too, how many stories these little maps tell and how many memories they evoke. I am remembering pedaling up Soapstone grade the day we met our good friend Steve, and how Cuyamaca's mountains and meadows smelled of pine and fern and flowers. I remember trespass adventures on the Irvine Ranch property, epic rides in the mountains behind Fallbrook, long expeditions on bike trails and roads to the farthest stretches of Orange County. It's especially fun to discover Monte's little reminders for me, such as these from a map of the hills behind Laguna: "road that you and Alice ride on" or "place where my mother took that picture of you and Miranda"....

In her 1942 memoir *West With The Night*, aviator Beryl Markham expressed her own fondness for maps with these words: "A map says to you, read me carefully, follow me closely, doubt me not...I am the earth in the palm of your hand...without me you are alone and lost."

I didn't feel alone or lost when I carried Monte's maps, his familiar handwriting having demystified the segment of world I was about to navigate. I like maps in general... the colors of them, the overview one couldn't otherwise grasp, the revelations of how the pieces fit together and where you are in the scheme of things. I like journeys plotted out with fingers and marked in felt tip pen, and I like contemplating the shape of land and water and the ways in which they meet. I like how maps enable us to soar above a place in order to become more truly part of it.

Most of all, I like knowing that someone made me a collection of customized maps to tuck into my backpack. I need no further evidence that I have been loved.

Recalibrate

In the dark hours before dawn one fateful October day, my sister's twenty-two-year-old son Ian crashed his car directly into a wall at a high rate of speed, with police in pursuit. He was airlifted to a nearby medical center where he spent many weeks on life support, in a coma, with massive and devastating brain damage. An MRI of his head revealed swelling, bleeding, and diffuse axonal injury caused by the traumatic shearing force of impact—meaning damage so widespread it would be impossible to pinpoint the areas and functions affected, and as if that weren't enough, he had a subsequent brain hemorrhage while still in the ICU. I didn't think he would make it and wasn't even sure that it was in his best interest to survive. One social worker put it this way: "Whoever he was, the Ian you knew is gone forever."

It was an epic tragedy that unleashed unmitigated misery and spilled into other lives, including my own. It broke my heart to contemplate the many experiences Ian would never have, the unmet potential and lost possibilities. One neurosurgeon declared the situation hopeless...end of life, he said...and it *was* a death, complicated by the fact that it wasn't, an ambiguity that imparted a special kind of cruelty to the nightmare. My sister, distraught and suicidal, kept a constant bedside vigil, her terrible grief understandable, but often she was angry and demanding. "If we had a normal family," she said more than once, "everyone would be right here taking shifts and helping me out."

Especially me. Decades and realities seemed to have faded, and in her eyes I was the big sister again, a fixer and rescuer, the one you could count on. I swallowed some of this old mythology and struggled with how much and how little I could reasonably do. My sister pointed out what an easy life I had, what a lucky life, and I believe that our fates involve choices as well as luck, but I briefly put my lucky life on hold and tried to help her, soon realizing that it could never be enough. I starting seeing a therapist who told me about boundaries, a concept I'd somehow missed in my upbringing, and this was useful, but I do have porous borders. I internalized the sadness, jumped whenever the phone rang, and lay awake at night, unable to push it out of my mind. The lack of resolution and relentless ramifications were overwhelming, and it wasn't my problem, but how does one turn away?

Even after he opened his eyes, Ian spent his days lying in the hospital bed, gazing emptily into space; he was unable to move of his own volition, could not follow instructions, and had no voice. We were advised that the key would be to recalibrate: change expectations, adjust ideas of progress, stop replaying what had happened and proceed with whatever there is. This was good advice, a modest strategy for coping with a long-term situation that seemed unfathomably bleak.

Sometimes I sang a childhood song to him, having read that the brain retains musical connections, and I talked to him, choosing big concrete brightly colored nouns and simple narratives. Remember trees, and a white moon in the sky? Remember the splash and sparkle of the swimming pool? Remember walking up the steps to your house, opening the door, and seeing that funny cat, Smoky?

Then one morning when I mentioned Smoky, Ian smiled. It was about five months after the accident, and he was still helpless and immobile in his hospital bed, but this was a broad, unequivocal grin, clearly connected to the cat. My sister had earlier claimed that he was able to grasp a pen and was beginning to write random numbers, letters, maybe words, and I'll admit that I was dubious, but now seemed a good moment to put it to the test. I placed a marker pen in his hand and a notebook under it and asked him if he wanted to write something. He took the pen purposefully, and staring straight ahead, without even looking at the page, he printed out three words: *I love you.*

It utterly took my breath away. He was still mute, but he'd given us a link; there was unequivocal evidence now of presence and sense. And could there be three words more compelling, poignant, earth shattering, miraculous, or heartbreaking? Oh, maybe it was just a piece of the song I had been singing. Maybe it's what he'd heard being said to him over and over for the last five months. But maybe it truly was what he wanted most to say…to anyone…to the world. I am. I feel. Connect to me. *I love you.*

Language. Meaning. Everything changed with those words. No one knew when or if he would coordinate fragments into consistent and cohesive sense, or summon skills as needed, or walk again, or speak. It's impossible even today to predict what the big picture holds or what kind of life he might yet have. But the universe shifted when language returned.

Months passed. If you recalibrated, then Ian's transfer from the hospital to a skilled care facility could be viewed as a triumph, and I was pleased to visit him in this new setting. He responded to his name when I greeted him, and he grinned that now familiar grin— goofy, off-kilter, and endearing. We looked at pictures of dogs in a magazine, and he smiled and turned the pages, and I suppose it's strange that I saw the turning of pages in a magazine as an accomplishment, but in this context, it *was*. I had recalibrated, as we all do over time, and as we must.

On a later visit, I found him sitting with other residents at a long table playing bingo. I pulled up a chair and sat alongside him, reminding him to look at his card, sometimes pointing to the correct column and repeating the number, pleased when he went to the right one and slid the little red plastic tab across it, another achievement. There was music in the background, a mix of catchy pop tunes from the sixties, songs that were played on radios so incessantly over the years that even now they slipped easily into my head. I was surprised at how quickly and thoroughly I still remembered lyrics, even to songs I disliked, and I wasn't the only one. Several residents, at least those over sixty, were singing and swaying back and forth to the *Age of Aquarius* as they tended to their bingo cards. Meanwhile the bingo caller, Hispanic and pretty, continued to chirp the numbers and write them on a board, and I rooted for my nephew and guided him gently when needed, and the music in the background filled the air like weather, a snowstorm of sugar.

When a Dionne Warwick song came on, I started singing too, rather close to the kid's ear. "Sorry about that, Ian," I said. "I know I'm not much of a singer." He smiled agreeably. His fingers found their way to a few more called numbers, and he slid the red tabs over, getting very close to bingo in at least two different rows. On my right was a fellow I'd seen here before writing tidy columns of numbers and sums in a notebook with intense concentration; now he was listening attentively, filling his card, numerically at ease. On *his* right, a plump woman adorned with hair bows and a sparkly necklace was clearly on a winning streak, racking up bingos and gaily singing along.

Eventually, almost everybody had won a game or two, including Ian. I motioned excitedly to his card. "Can you say bingo, Ian?" asked the bingo-calling girl. "No," he said, proudly. No had become his out-loud word. It's a short and limiting one, but a word nonetheless, and a *voice*, oh it was so good to hear a voice after months of silence, even if just a syllable's worth. I kept thinking of where he had so recently been, that state of suspended animation, the non-responsive staring into space. It was humbling now to see him transfer from bed to wheelchair, walk a few steps with a cane, respond to humor, give a high five.

At times the tragedy of it still colored everything. He's twenty-two and shouldn't be in a place like this, I thought, and unbidden images kept coming to me of Humpty Dumpty's tumble from the wall, of irrevocable brokenness that no one could ever piece together. But it's poisonous to dwell on all the should-haves and wish-he-hadn'ts. We are given only this unexpected present and whatever ambiguous outcomes it may yield.

I reminded myself too that the human brain is a vast and complex mystery, a universe we are only beginning to explore. Why give more credence to ominous-sounding commentators than to evidence for potential? Who would have predicted even this much progress? The young are resilient, and no two brains, or brain injuries, are alike. Who knows how much can be recovered?

So Simon and Garfunkel were singing *Feelin' Groovy*, and here I was, making grand allowances for hope, but somewhere in the middle of "Life I love you…all is groovy" an officious young administrator called me over for an on-the-run conference in a corner of the multipurpose room. "I'm not telling you anything I haven't told your sister," she said, "but she needs to give me a discharge plan for Ian."

Actually, she said all sorts of things, but that was the essence of it. She was smaller than me even in her high-heeled shoes, and her black hair was pulled back tightly from her forehead, and she reminded me of a student who doesn't know the answer to a question and is going to bluff her way through. I told her the truth, which is that my sister had been doing everything humanly possible to figure this out. I asked if there was someone who could advise and help her.

"We've told her what she needs to do," she said, which didn't sound the same as helping. She was trying to be business-like, I know, but she was the kind of person who wouldn't look you straight in the eye. She was very young but she had a deflating effect on me, and I felt that there were lessons in gentleness and heart that life had not yet taught her.

I went back to Ian, who had been presented with a basket of bingo prizes from which to choose, mostly ties and toiletries. The girls were trying to sell him on a bright shiny bicycle bell for his wheelchair and I completely understood his refusal. I urged him to choose something for his mom instead, and he selected a tiny blue atomizer of cologne. I handed him a magazine to look at while he waited for lunch. It was an animal magazine, a good one with some excellent pictures of cats, and he immediately began to turn the pages and look at the images. I hugged him and left.

Nearly two years have gone by since the car crash. Ian lives at home now with his mother, whose life consists largely of care giving, and attends a rehabilitation program on weekdays. One can only imagine how he perceives the world, what history he recalls, or what concepts he truly grasps, but he walks and speaks and affably interacts, and even if his improvement is not linear or consistent, he seems to be rewiring pathways. He has a visible scar along his head, but he looks handsome, his dark brows emphasizing a pure gaze and ready smile. There's an essence and flicker of the person he was, but he mostly seems reborn, an innocent being, responsive and alive in the present. Great challenges persist, and it's an unending fight, but at the heart of him he seems happy and secure. He must surely know he's loved.

And it's not my story, but there it is. Blood and history and the aching of my heart connect me to it, and I've struggled to understand and tried to help. I finally saw it was essential that I walk away and refocus on my own life, but it's a story that continues. It can be a constant source of sadness or a new font of faith. I recalibrate as needed.

So This Is Christmas

ⵊ

I went to visit my mother and found her in the multipurpose room of her assisted living facility watching an old Andy Williams Christmas special. Maybe you remember those? The stage is sparkling with fake snow and everyone is wearing scarves and bright holiday sweaters, and Andy is crooning about the kind of Christmases not a one of us has ever had. After songs about chestnuts, sleigh bells, and jolly old Saint Nick, along comes a frisky quartet of tap-dancing reindeer and I'm not sure whether to laugh or groan, but when I look around the room, everyone seems transfixed. This stuff is like a drug.

I turn my attention back to the screen and focus on Andy. He looks rather dapper, in a mummified way, as he engages in a bit of banter with a Nashville-style singer dressed as a snow queen in a cloak and white stretch pants. After Andy and the Snow Queen do a number, the Osmond Brothers join the fun, and then a full-on choir as the spectacle tilts back and forth between secular whimsy and religious inspiration. Eventually an assemblage of children joins Andy on stage by the Christmas tree to add their voices to the joyful noise. They are groomed to perfection in their holiday attire; you can almost smell the shampoo. Now and then the spotlights sweep across the audience, which looks eerily like the Republican National Convention of August '08, and I'm trying to guess when this thing was made. If memory serves, the variety show Christmas special seems to have achieved the height of its popularity in the '60s and '70s, but this one could be as recent as the early 1980s, judging by the bigness of the hair and the post-disco, early Reagan-era bling. A possible clue: the four Osmonds report having sired a combined total of forty-five sons and daughters at this point. Maybe we can roughly date it from there.

It's funny to be sitting here next to my mother watching this. I wonder if it brings her back to a certain living room in another time and place. "Escapist, manipulative corn," my father might have said, but if it worked on us at all, what it stirred up was not sentiment but dissatisfaction and envy, for we saw nothing of ourselves in these concoctions. Did everyone but us experience this kind of heartwarming gaiety at Christmas? In time, we would come to understand that the vague discontent was deliberately provoked. We would see that our culture was designed to create a chronic sense of emptiness that could never be quenched, that it transformed everything into wanting.

But in that long ago Long Island living room, we were simply innocents watching. The little black and white television screen was a flickering window to something false and silly, but it gathered us together sometimes as though before a hearth. My mother remembers those as happy days, and I will never take that illusion away from her. But does she ever feel the ache in the gap between what she wanted and what was? Between what was and what is? She just seems glad I am here to enjoy the show with her.

Outside the talk is of shopper stampedes and shootings in stores, deflation and recession, terrorist attacks real and anticipated, disturbing uncertainties. Yesterday I ventured into a mall on Santa Ana's version of Main Street, bleaker than usual despite the seasonal soundtrack. At one point I heard John Lennon's voice singing his song about *Happy Christmas, War Is Over* and it made me so sad I stopped dead in my tracks. What is wrong with me?

And so this is Christmas
I hope you have fun
The near and the dear one
The old and the young...

I remember singing Christmas carols. I remember believing in the meaning, pure and uncorrupted. Now, appalled but oddly tranquilized, I sit in the multipurpose room with my small white-haired mother and a sundry assortment of other souls, all of us nostalgic for what we never had, together in our yearning.

While Venus Passed

While Venus was in transit across the sun, I was on my knees in a shoe store helping my elderly mother try on shoes. The wonder of the former is obvious. The wonder in the latter situation was the mere fact that my mother had gone along with the idea of buying new shoes, an action which involves two things that upset her: a change in what is familiar, and the expenditure of money. She gets attached to whatever she already has, no matter its condition, *and* she is apparently stuck at some point in the old days when things were priced as she believes they should be, when a perfectly fine pair of shoes, for example, might set you back two bucks—that's her scale. So whenever we attempt any kind of shopping, one key to success is to prevent her from seeing the prices. It's also helpful to tell her that everything is on sale. Anyway, she had agreed to get new shoes, and Venus was in transit across the sun, and I was on the floor of an Orange County shoe store.

It was an unpleasant and humbling task. I once read in an article by a gerontologist that the condition of the feet is an excellent indicator of an elderly person's general well being and the care he or she is receiving. Not such good scores here. When I peeled away her socks, damp and stained with various oozings, I saw inflammation and neglect and desiccated yellow nails on twisted toes. She had a gash on her left ankle protected by a napkin that she had tucked into the sock. I bought soft new socks for her and discreetly threw the old ones in the trash, and after several attempts, tentative hobbling around, and a few loud squeals of excitement, we finally managed to find a comfortable pair of shoes. She proclaimed them feminine because instead of shoelaces there were Velcro straps, Mary Jane style, and she liked the fact that they were open on top and didn't cut into the sore part of her bone as her others had apparently been doing.

Those old bones are as brittle as glass, and she'd recently fallen again and broken her arm, but she still walks too fast, swinging her cane randomly and at great peril to anyone nearby. She wears a hearing aid but is profoundly deaf, and I imagine it's like being underwater, voices drowned into indistinct murmurs sounding very far away. One day I bought her a pair of big cushiony headphones to amplify the volume and filter out ambient noise when she watched TV in her room, and I thought it would be an amazing breakthrough for her to be able to hear as well as watch, but it didn't really help much and she couldn't adapt, so she wrapped up the headphones in toilet paper and hid them in her drawer, and I was again reminded of the myth of Sisyphus and the folly of taking that on. I stepped back and let it go, and that's how I've learned to cope. Why make life more complicated by trying to force my sensibilities onto her?

Shoe purchase completed, I took her out for ice cream and a stop at the Dollar Store. We had a fine shopping spree: colorful hair ties, a purple hairbrush, scotch tape and new sunglasses. Her battiness has become sort of funny and benign, and she's generally pretty cheerful. She asked me why she was feeling so old. "Maybe because you're almost ninety," I said, which actually means I wrote that down on paper, because, as I mentioned, she's deaf, although she always insists she can hear me. She was surprised to learn how old she is. (Maybe we're always surprised.)

I had hoped to discard her old shoes, but when we got back to her room I had to placate her by stashing them in the closet. Then I detoured to the office to request a podiatry visit and a more diligent routine of washing, and I left with a tiny sense of accomplishment, fleeting though it may be. The point is, sometimes that's all you can hope for. I have lately had the feeling that my mother is on some secret voyage of her own, as perhaps she always was, and it seems to me there's something touchingly brave about her. I picture her now, her thick white hair in a single braid, wearing a bright red polyester jacket with a pink or yellow shirt, adorned with shiny Mardi Gras beads, a big-faced watch that long ago stopped, and a silver Star of David. Her room is crammed with books that she no longer reads but I think they keep her company, and at night she sings herself to sleep to dream of days she thinks were happy. I hope someday that's how she'll leave, sailing peacefully away in a dream like that.

That evening, Monte and I went for a walk in the old town district of Orange. Because we always vote early by mail, I'd forgotten that it happened to be election day, and I was surprised by the sight of the theater turned church turned polling place, its doors still open, citizens within casting their votes behind curtains at the end of the day. The voting sign pointing straight to the cross did give me pause, but there's always something affirmative about seeing people tending to their civic duties. Sure, the political scene was contentious and economic reports dire, but in the gold waning light it was easy to feel for a moment that things would be okay.

People were out and about, socializing at tables along the street and strolling around the plaza. Earlier I had resisted ice cream but now succumbed to a celebratory macaroon from a glass display case of baked goods at Watson's Drug and Soda Fountain. We paused to look up at the old fruit exchange building, peered into stores all a'jumble with stuff, and noticed a sign for up-dos at the beauty school. A red-haired woman in a polka dot dress pushed along a baby stroller, an old man in Bermuda shorts was walking his poodle, three boys in scout uniforms made a beeline for the candy store. Across the street a row of windows with blue awnings were lined up wide-eyed against an indigo sky. A celestial event had transpired that would not occur again within our lifetimes. I don't mind knowing I spent my day on the planet trying to be kind, glimpsing democracy in action, walking the evening streets with someone I love, and eating a macaroon. I don't mind at all.

Octobers

Late in the day I rode my bicycle along the main road to the old ranch house, where Monte was at a meeting that would (supposedly) soon adjourn. The tide was low and the beach was empty, and at Las Panoches, a cluster of balloons had sprung from a post like a bouquet...turn here for a party, I guess. Nearby a cow was grazing with a tiny new-to-the world black calf at her side. Several deer loitered beneath the eucalyptus trees where the road rises and briefly divides, and the hazy light turned rose-gold. At the turnoff to the house I rode through the orchard in the hopes of gathering some persimmons ripe enough to make pudding, but somebody had beat me to it. I saw a few high up in the branches, placed my bike on the grass, and tried to jump and grab them, but they were far out of reach. My friend Kit happened to come by—his wife was at the meeting too—and offered his assessment.

"Why don't you just climb up?" he asked. But I've never climbed a tree, I said, and anyway, those don't look like they're worth climbing after, and Kit conceded the point. He managed to reach up high and pluck one that was ready to fall, and then we shook the branches with no success but found another on the ground, as soft as jam and half-consumed by other kinds of creatures. There would be no persimmon pudding. Instead I stood beneath the yellow-orange leaves and swallowed a morsel of persimmon-sweetness, receiving communion, communing with fall.

I chose to stay outdoors and wait. Through the windows, I saw neighbors gathered at a table in the warm glow of interior light, a community discussion, local democracy in action...it was a good thing, but I pulled a book from my pack and sat on the porch steps next to someone's patient dog and gazed outward into the green and the shadows. October has almost fled, I thought. A couple of weeks ago we were in New York, and the days were as hot as summer's furnace core, and now I'd been hearing that Northeastern storms were approaching, with perhaps an early snowfall. Time slides around, its pacing erratic, its line-up capricious. But the light of October has a certain slant always, an angle auguring loss.

On this very date in 1971 I was in Chicago getting married at the Cook County Courthouse on Clark Street. "Get under the flag," said the judge, and I couldn't shake the image of the flag as a blanket to crawl under, and I started to giggle because I was already hysterical, and the judge scolded me and said this wasn't a joke, young lady. The groom was a medical student who wore faded purple bell-bottoms, and I was a dark-haired girl in a very short dress, and after being married we walked downtown and through Lincoln Park where trees were dropping yellow leaves, and at night the other medical students made us a spaghetti dinner celebration in a shabby brownstone building that served as a fraternity house. I went outside and sat on those other steps, and I cried because I thought my life was over.

Oh, it most assuredly was not. I had placed myself in suspension for a while, but I eventually came to see that many endings yield to new beginnings and sometimes astonishing outcomes. Everything that happened or didn't happen has led me to here, I thought, where I am sitting on the porch of a grand old house on a California cattle ranch with a book on my lap watching night enter a garden. Behind me a handful of diligent citizens, my husband among them, are gathered at a table in a lamp-lit common room, constructively discussing or spinning their wheels, but affirmatively engaged in community and living. I'm a late arrival, connected to this and apart from it too, and with an outsider's perspective, I contemplate.

Earlier in the day I'd ventured into town and had coffee with Laura, my Italian-teacher-who-became-my-friend. Laura grew up in Rome within view of the Vatican and studied enough Catholicism to be skeptical. "It's people I believe in," she told me... but she prays anyway. She prays when she walks the dog, when she puts clothes on the line to dry, when she watches her grandson play with his trains. "You pray too," she said, "even if you think you don't know how." I do, I thought. And I am. Some aftertaste of persimmon still sweetens my tongue and the autumn light drifts into dusk and my heart beats its mantra of thanks.

The worst October was when my father died. It was 1978, and that first marriage was over. I was a graduate student by then, living in Syracuse with an alcoholic professor ten years my senior. The bed in which I slept faced a window with a view of the top of a great maple tree; I remember the dissonant beauty of its bright leaves on the morning when I got the news. My car was low on gas, my wallet empty of cash, and the alcoholic professor handed me six dollars and told me I could add it to my bill.

Don't worry. I was free of him. I picked up my sister in Cortland, a half-hour to the south, and drove to Long Island to face the new reality that had been so abruptly delivered to us. "Only one thing counts," my father had said, "who loves you, and how well."

Even now, I sometimes get a brand new pang of missing him so sharp and sudden it almost makes me gasp. He had dark eyes and black hair, spoke poems and stood straight, and on the day he died, at the age of sixty-seven, he was still working hard. He used to tell us he was a fighter, a fighter tied up, and if only he could free himself, he could fight some more. He saw his life as a battlefield, and he tried to protect his children but knew that we bore the scars of discord. *The clock is ticking*, he always said, and time indeed did flee, but the promises of *domani* never came.

"Someday all that we do now will belong to a dream..." he wrote in a letter to his brother in 1944.

It feels like a dream I'm still dreaming.

The meeting concludes, the cool air is infused with talk and greetings, and the patient dog finds his person. Monte puts my bike in the back of the car and we head home together, but first we stop to look at the crescent moon rising in the sky above the cove, and the light of a distant fishing boat glowing like a lantern, faint and true. Shall I see it as a symbol? Do we imbue the world with meaning? All I know is that if you just keep putting one foot in front of the other, eventually you're on some sort of journey. Somehow I found my way here, where persimmons grow and cows graze and none of it should have logically ensued from where I started, but that's the way dreams are. And it's October again.

Transplant

Even the oldest stories inhabit the present—even here, so far from where they happened—and the writing of them begins in the physical world, in sensory input and concrete nouns. I shall start, then, by telling you that the sea looks slate gray this morning, and a white sky has smudged the outline of Santa Rosa Island, and the radio on the kitchen counter is playing *Morning Edition*. There is a mug of strong coffee at my elbow, a slice of pumpkin pie on a plate, and a bowl of fruit at the center of a plain wood table illuminated by a tentative slant of sunlight. The moment gleams; everything has its own import and gravity. But the moment belongs to a year that is drawing to a close. I can almost feel the whoosh in my ear as it rushes by me, and I want to rise and rouse myself before it's gone, but I am sick and stalled. My diagnosis: bad cold. It's a trifle of an ailment, but it has sapped my energy all week and driven me indoors where I keep bumping into memories of someone I loved, someone who lived with infirmity every day of her life.

She was Marlene, my history and my heart, the sister with the honey hair who followed me like a gossamer shadow, seeing me much finer than I was. We walked to school together in hand-me-down dresses, ate lemon ice in pleated cups beneath the el, danced in a swath of kitchen light that swept into the living room and transformed it to a stage. We sat on the hot summer sidewalk of Coney Island Avenue with a pot of water and an ordinary umbrella, pretending we were at the beach, evoking pity from passersby but perfectly content. One day we purloined a hefty wedge of layer cake from the refrigerator—it was an Ebinger's bakery cake, the kind with mocha frosting and thinly slivered almonds. We wrapped it in a bandanna that I tied to a stick and slung hobo-style over my shoulder...and we ran away together. Rain began to pelt the city streets before we even reached the corner, and we took shelter in the doorway of *Tobin's Furs* where three pale plaster mannequins stood in the window, chipped and barefooted, forever on tiptoes, wearing mink coats. That's as far as we went. We ate the cake and wondered if anyone would notice that we had finally run away. It wasn't much of an adventure, I suppose, but I've held that image for all these many years: my sister and I, huddled in the doorway, watching the rain. We kept each other safe back then.

I knew little but understood much, in the way that children do. I had grown up aware that two of my siblings had kidney disease, but I didn't really know what it was. In a family where angry and explicit words were hurled through the air like flaming spears and no day ended without tirades and tears or some calamitous last straw that threatened to send all six of us kids to foster homes, the existence and nature of this congenital disease were surprisingly unacknowledged and unarticulated. What I gleaned was that although Marlene and my brother Eddie *looked* fine, something inside their bodies didn't properly work. My sister's case was apparently more pronounced, although Eddie's condition would deteriorate over time.

And so, in the course of our childhoods, Marlene was often the subject of concerned murmurings, but even a practiced eavesdropper like myself could not quite decipher them. She was implicitly granted a bit of leeway, mostly in the form of lower expectations, and was periodically banished to a hospital from which she sent letters in her little-girl writing that spoke of her ordeals and her yearning to come home. I missed her during those absences, and I walked around with a sad feeling inside that never went away, but somehow I got used to the pattern, just as I would get used to hearing of her struggles in the ensuing years. I came to accept her limitations in a way she perhaps never did; some of us were healthy, some of us were not. I felt guilty sometimes for being the one who wasn't sick, born right between a brother and a sister who were, but not being sick was a fundamental part of my identity. I guess I'd won the lottery.

When Marlene was seventeen and in her last year of high school on Long Island, her kidneys entirely ceased to function. She had been losing weight—at first I actually thought it was intentional, for she was suddenly thin in the way we believed we were supposed to be — but she was also becoming alarmingly weak. When she continued to refuse food, I thought this starvation diet had gone too far. "Enough is enough," I said, in my bossy big sister way, trying to bribe her with Chinese take-out. Pretty soon she could barely stumble from her bed, and we brought her to a hospital, where a doctor said, "Renal failure. This girl needs immediate dialysis. Lethargy has set in." I had never heard of renal failure, dialysis, or even lethargy.

And so began my sister's life on machines and transplant lists. But I was in my twenties by then, and basically gone…various colleges in upstate New York, a short-lived marriage in Chicago, Greyhound buses, furnished rooms…some of it made sense, much of it did not. I was trying to live a life, I guess, but mostly I was fleeing from a house of pain and tumult that had only become more overwhelming. It wasn't just the kidney disease; there was mental illness, constant fighting and volatility, a scarcity of money and the buffers it provides. No one was unscathed, not even the healthy ones. My father shelved his dreams and worked too hard trying to keep us all going, but his burdens were extraordinary. I was the oldest daughter. I wanted to be a good person, and I tried for a while, but it was too big to fix and too hard to watch. I had to leave to discover who I was, or even *if* I was. I wasn't sure about anything.

In the course of a dozen years Marlene endured three kidney transplants. Two were immediately rejected, including one from my mother, but another, a cadaver kidney from a child, proved lucky—it functioned for eight years. My sister's body was distorted and scarred, her daily life included a daunting lineup of drugs, and she was never what one would call healthy, but she was free of the machine, and those eight years were good ones. There had been talk sometimes of me as a potential donor, but other kidneys had materialized, and although I liked to think I would have been willing, no one ever asked. When the eight-year kidney finally ceased to function, my sister went back on dialysis, and I think there was one more attempt at transplant with a cadaver kidney, but it did not go well. And by now I was in California.

Ah, California. I felt that I had found a home at last, a new beginning at the age of thirty-one, still young. I'd always had fantasies about California, and now I learned to love the sassafras scent of chaparral, the sun-bleached hills in multiple auburn hues, the hot dry winds that stirred up something new in me, something dormant that wanted to awaken. It was the sky that first suggested that my life belonged to me. My own skin said it felt good to feel good. My heart pointed me towards a happier kind of love, to the possibility of a different kind of family. I knew I could not purge myself of all the sadness I was carrying, and I knew there were people who missed me and needed me, but I wanted to see what the world could be, and I wanted to be in it. "It's natural and healthy," said a therapist I'd gone to for advice. "A living thing reaches for the light." I already knew there was no going back.

I never gave a kidney. I write that with remorse and shame. It's a fact that I have lived with for many years now, and I wish I could undo it. How much are we responsible for one another? More than I ever knew.

But it wasn't that simple. The request came as I was settling into my new life, and I agonized about it. I did research and made phone calls and talked to doctors and transplant coordinators, donors and recipients. I had never heard of anyone having five transplants, and I wondered if my sister's medical history might diminish the chances of success. I had begun to wish I might someday have a child, and I wondered if being short one kidney might make a pregnancy more difficult. And I was scared. Yes, I was scared. I asked for more time to think about it. Marlene felt I was being callous and cruel. "It was always understood that you would give me a kidney," she said, which was a surprise to me. She demanded an answer right away. I resented her demand.

For a long time, we were estranged. "You had a chance to spare me from a life of suffering," she told me, "but you condemned me instead." I believed this. A few years later, having made a patchy peace with her, having visited often and watched her in decline, having had a baby and blessings in abundance, I offered to give her my kidney. And I meant it.

But I asked her to come to California for the transplant, and I think I had a certain time frame in mind. There was an excellent medical center nearby, and the staff told me reassuringly that there had been many improvements in organ transplantation and anti-rejection drugs since I had first contemplated this, and I was still afraid, but I was ready at last—it was my destiny and I would face it. It was the right thing and the only thing to do.

My sister's response stunned me. "*I'm* the one who's sick," she said. "How *dare* you call me up at your convenience and present all these conditions? You never understood that this was supposed to be an expression of unconditional love. You've always promised so much and delivered so little."

Maybe she didn't mean it. Maybe she wouldn't have said it if she hadn't been in pain. Maybe it isn't true. But the roster of my failures and mistakes is a lengthy one, I must admit, and I have learned to live with useless guilt and the acid dripping of old regrets. I know that I have loved and love deeply, but perhaps I did not have the gift for loving fully. My self-protective instinct overshadowed my impulse for sacrifice, and the years have fled, and suddenly I am a sixty-year-old insomniac, organs intact, playing things back. Time teaches but does not assuage. I guess everything comes down to kindness and forgiveness.

And yet, even after that awful conversation, Marlene and I eventually reclaimed some shaky ground and continued to communicate. She lived with her husband in Florida and spent hours of every day attached to a home dialysis machine. I was thriving, transplanted three thousand miles away. But there was a fundamental bond between us, no matter what, and we didn't want to lose each other entirely. I think I was almost forgiven, by her if not myself.

The last time we really talked was on New Year's Day, 2000. I was sick then, too, recovering in bed from the worst flu I'd ever had, waking up intermittently to glimpses on a television screen of what seemed a surreal series of ceremonial dances and celebrations marking the start of the new millennium as it crawled from East to West across the planet. When Marlene called, I took the phone to the window seat and sat there visiting with her for a long time. We laughed about all the extravagant pomp and anxiety that had accompanied this particular turning of the digits, and we chatted about Frank McCourt's newest book, and then waxed nostalgic about things we both remembered from long ago days, things no one else would understand. Oh, how we laughed! And maybe the residue of illness had sensitized me, or maybe it was just the advent of a brand new year, but we seemed to have reached a defining moment, and I realized with great clarity how much she meant to me, and how dear and irreplaceable she was, and I sensed she might be feeling the same way about me.

Three weeks later, she was gone. It should not have seemed sudden, but it did. I wasn't even there.

On this white sky day, I wonder. Do we own our fleeting lives? Do we leave because we can? Will years of penance finally yield to peace? May I accept the balm that is the beauty of the world? My sister seems to be sitting across the table in this house she never entered, letting me figure it out for myself. Outside, the ceanothus is blossoming early, looking like lace, and a small brown wren is perched on a branch, and the road is gray and leading into nowhere. I am swept into a gust of time; I can barely write these words.

The Open Road

We are somewhere on Highway 6 in Nevada, miles and miles of straight road edged by scrubby desert and barren mountains. I have my feet on the dashboard and I'm chewing gum and scrolling through the playlists on Monte's iPod. We're in a silver van that we've rented just for this adventure, and it's our second day of driving, maybe our third. It's just the two of us on the open road. "You're getting bored," says Monte.

"I am not," I say.

But if you're going to take a trip like this, you better enjoy the ramblings of your own mind. Unfortunately, I don't. For starters, I'm obsessing about the fact that we left our old dog at the Humane Society kennel, and I've convinced myself that she is traumatized and grief-stricken in this terrible abandonment. I have already called the staff twice to see how she is and to remind them to comfort her. "She's doing fine," said the woman at the desk, "but she can't come to the phone right now." Cute. And I would call again anyway, but we're not getting cell service here.

Driving into Bakersfield yesterday we passed white barren hills, an occasional oil well, cottonwood trees and old barns. There was a Hay for Sale sign…Siesta Apartments…a boarded up restaurant…so many brave little businesses gone under…and me meanwhile bereft about the dog. Later we stopped near Kernville for gas and a market. A skinny sun-dried woman in a t-shirt and tattoos stood by a motorcycle and smoked a cigarette, looking as though she'd been around the block way more than once and it wasn't that great. A couple of doughy-looking teen-aged girls with penciled-in eyebrows were standing around in a parking lot watching for their prince, and an old guy with an unruly beard was taking his change in lottery tickets at the gas station.

"I'm gonna go for the mega-million this time," he told the clerk, sounding pretty confident. In front of the grocery store a little girl in purple hot pants and chunky high black boots stood over a cardboard box filled with mewing kittens, hoping to give them away, no takers so far.

Naturally it made me think of the dog.

The road got twistier and I started to get a little carsick, plus my ears were popping, so I put away my journal for awhile, but not before recording the image of Monte slipping off his flip-flops and balancing on the rocks in the Kern River just so he could put his feet in and feel the temperature of the water because, as he explained, that's what he has to do. He also likes to get the lay of the land as we drive, composing an ongoing sort of inquiry and commentary on the physical aspects of the world: "This was all greened up and forested when I came here with Steve, all covered in timber. I can't believe how far this fire burned. Did it jump the highway back there? Check out that switchback. Where does it go? Look at that interesting rock formation. You can tell they recently resurfaced this road. Is that a waterfall over there?"

We were climbing along Sherman Pass at about 6,000 feet, and the air was clean and cool. There were light colored rock formations, the charred sticks of bare trees, and yellow blooming brush everywhere. I wish I knew the name of those flowers. I wish I'd brought along a field guide so I could look it up. I wish there was a bottle of root beer in the cooler. Yeah. Root beer. It's a little different. I'm really not that into Coke lately. I definitely intend to give up Diet Cokes. Those artificial sweeteners can't be good for you. I wonder why sugar gets such a bad rap anyway?

Sugar. Now there's a thought. Maybe we still have some of that chocolate. Okay. Let's see what this satellite radio has to offer. Two stations of Sinatra? Three of Howard

Stern? How about Coffee House? Best of the Seventies, perhaps? CNN? NPR? BBC? Are we there yet?

There, however, is here. We park and walk a short pleasant stretch of the Pacific Crest Trail along the south fork of the Kern River in the Southern Sierra wilderness.

Our first night camping was at Tuttle Creek, outside of Lone Pine, a place where we often stayed in the 1980s when we were younger, fitter versions of ourselves. Monte promptly clicked into full-on camping mode. I think he genuinely enjoys this—there's an order and compactness to it that suits him. For me, though, it's a sentence. I hate having to think ahead about every detail, then lie there cramped and still in our metal receptacle hoping for sleep. I hate having to climb outside in the dark to go pee. I hate using nylon sleeping bags—blankets should not swish and slip off in the night. Mostly, I hate the landscape of my mind, despite the full moon rising over the mountains, a big round yellow disk.

In the morning we passed Manzanar...sorrow in the air...snow in the high mountains...a wide panorama...a starting over...a day blue and white and clean. On the radio, R.E.M. is singing *It's the End of the World as We Know It*. Onward to Bishop and beyond to Highway 6 and Great Basin and Salt Lake City and southern Utah...

"I have seen almost more beauty than I can bear," wrote Everett Ruess, who vanished into the Utah wilderness when he was twenty years old, and even as shallow as I am, I *do* know what he meant. I won't cheapen the wonders with words. But my reverence for beauty diminishes with strong cold winds, and a snowy landscape looks best to me from a vantage point with heat. In this I differ from the woman we met at an overlook near Wheeler Peak the morning after snow who actually mimed some sort of swoosh-swoosh ski motion and said, "Yes, yes! I smell winter sports!"

So I'm a hotel person, basically. What's wrong with that? And I love nature as much as the next guy, but I definitely crave the material comforts and distractions of a city now and then. And I have had a headache from the altitude ever since our little stroll to Baker Lake, somewhere above 10,000 feet, unbearably beautiful indeed. And I'm thinking about that funny little dog, transformed by age, who just wants to be near her people, knowing nothing of mortality but showing us the fast-forward version of our own. And I'm remembering a cross-country trip in 1974, calling home collect from KOA campgrounds in alien worlds…the befuddled voice of faraway Daddy, recipient of Georgia pecans and engorged phone bills…the ringing silence afterwards.

Blind Canyon. Outback Taxidermy. Sometimes the world looks empty. Lonely roads and abandoned dwellings. So many broken dreams. I wish I could have photographed that flag-draped trailer with junk in the yard, or the wooden house with the broken windows and laundry on the line, unlikely places, but someone is home.

On the radio an American Marine is talking about the difficulty of gouging out a man's eyeball during house-to-house fighting in Fallujah. On another station, the need for access to clean water in sub-Saharan Africa. Barack Obama not wearing his American flag lapel pin. Retreating ice in the Arctic Ocean. Blackwater shootings. Ethanol glut.

I wish I could shake the feeling that I am bearing witness to endings. I wish I could pause more often, as I have watched Monte do, to listen and be still. I wish I wouldn't stamp my own sad story on the world. I wish I could look inside and feel a sense of peace.

I reach back to fumble through the grocery sacks, remembering those sweet dried mission figs we bought at Trader Joe's. And I don't know if it's because of the personal season of life I'm in or the history that we are living—and it's probably both—but everything lately seems intense and unsettling, and the open road just opens up the onslaught.

"You're getting bored," says Monte.

"I am not," I say. And I'm not. I'm never bored, just a little overwhelmed, a little awed, a little baffled.

Smooth In The Water

We'll get this straight from the start. I do not know how to swim. Somehow I just found myself all grown up one day never having learned. People are always appalled when they discover this, as though I have been concealing some embarrassing deficiency that causes them to view me differently. Many, in fact, offer to correct it. I confessed my inability to a four-year-old boy named Troy once as I was tucking him into bed. He immediately sat up to show me how, paddling with his hands in the air above his bed and meticulously explaining the whole process. "So do you get it now?" he asked, leaning back against his pillows, touchingly pleased to have helped me. I didn't have the heart to say no.

I had attempted more traditional classes over the years—a few aborted sessions in a cold YMCA swimming pool in Chicago, and various lessons later on taught by robust athletic amphibians in Southern California. I never progressed much beyond pushing off from the side and propelling myself a few feet through the water. At some point I would inevitably freak out, thrash around, and swallow water, emerging with gasps and sputters. Fear was a stronger force than the occasional flicker of hope my miniscule successes engendered. Eventually the possibility of my becoming a swimmer seemed so remote I could no longer imagine it.

And then, just a few months ago, having resolved to grow and challenge myself, I decided to give it one more try. I signed up for lessons with a woman who teaches all the toddlers in the Santa Ynez Valley. I bought a bathing suit for the first time in decades – a modest black one, of course, the kind that's supposed to make you look ten pounds thinner but never does, and I padded out in flip-flops and sat watching in awe as a little girl in a pink bathing suit concluded her lesson by retrieving rings from the bottom of the pool, a stunt which inspired neither confidence nor enthusiasm in me. Her proud mom wrapped her in a towel and I watched the little show-off happily skip away, knowing I would not leave giggling.

Now it was my turn. I strapped on a pair of goggles that cut into the bridge of my nose and immersed myself tentatively. It was exactly as I remembered it – an alien and inhospitable environment that smelled of chlorine and danger. The instructor was patient and kind, trying initially to get a sense of my level of comfort or discomfort in the water. Wanting to please her, I immediately demonstrated my very best trick, the one where I push off from the side, extend my body, bravely put my face in the water, and sail across the width of the pool. I think it's fairly impressive, and I wish we could have left it at that. But then there predictably came the business of blowing bubbles. Things always deteriorate from the bubble-blowing point.

I endured two sessions of tedious kicking, of breathing exercises that usually morphed into hyperventilation, and of gliding toward the deep end of the pool on a kickboard straight into panic. I discovered again how much I hate holding my breath, and how little faith I place in liquid. I remembered how confused I get when I have to coordinate physical movements, especially with the fluster factor of knowing that to fail is to drown. I recognized, above all, how much I love the feel of ground beneath my feet, and I resolved to henceforth tread attentively and appreciatively on the earth. I reminded myself that no one was forcing me to do this, and hadn't I gotten along fine so far watching from the shore and avoiding small boats? I had given it a bit of a try, got my feet wet, so to speak. Now I quit. I hadn't even made it to minnow.

Naturally, I promptly turned this into a statement about my failure as a human being. Once again, I had started something and dropped the ball. It's a pattern that has worried me for years. And I'm pretty sure this was the last swimming class I will ever attempt; I cannot—and never will—swim.

But my friend Steve, who knows me well, said, "You don't give a crap about swimming. Why pretend?"

This was a liberating thought, and possibly true.

Ironically, the swimming instructor called me a few days later and said, "I don't know what's going on inside your head, Cynthia, but you would be a beautiful swimmer! You were smooth in the water. Smooth." Well, that's a new one for me.

The French philosopher Gaston Bachelard wrote: "The call of water demands a total offering, an inner offering. Water needs an inhabitant. It summons like a fatherland."

I too have heard its call and been swept along by its currents. Last night I dreamed I was in a gray foamy sea, and for the first time ever, I could feel that the water wasn't just pulling me down, it was pushing me up, rendering me buoyant. The ocean was vast, but I stayed horizontal and rose with the swell, breathing the sky, smooth in the water.

So I'll swim through my dreams, and perhaps that's good enough. Maybe maturity is accepting what we cannot do and inhabiting that reality, not with resignation but contentment.

The Planet Of The Young

"We'll just drive down to L.A."

Hearing my daughter speak those words reminds me that there's a fathomless gap between the world of twenty-somethings and the rest of us. "But it's already four o'clock," I observe unhelpfully.

"So what's your point, Mom?"

She was having some sort of crisis with her visa. This morning we took her to be fingerprinted at our local Application Support Office—who even knew there was such a place? It was a storefront facility with darkened windows located in a K-Mart parking lot between the Deluxe Nails and Waxing Salon and the Indo-Chinese take-out. Things were hushed and serious in the Application Support Office. There was a flag in the reception area, and on the wall a framed photograph of the President and a large sign forbidding cell phones, cameras, briefcases, tweezers, trench coats, chewing gum, whatever comes to mind. I decided to wait outside rather than forfeit so many of my possessions, so I don't exactly know what transpired in there, but my daughter emerged a half hour later with more papers and additional tasks. Apparently some crucial form now had to be filed and something official done to her passport, but said passport must somehow be back in her hands in time for her flight to London Monday, and there would be that long Fourth of July weekend coming up, which didn't help.

Not to worry. It turns out there are people you pay to expedite such things. (Again, I ask, who knew?) There is in fact a woman in Los Angeles who can get everything processed in time, guaranteed, but she needs all the papers before eight o'clock tomorrow morning. So my daughter casually suggests that she and her boyfriend simply borrow the car and head down to L.A., first driving thirty miles in the opposite direction to deposit me at home, then a hundred miles south to the house of the passport and visa expeditor, and then home again tonight.

It's inconvenient, sure, but certainly not insurmountable, so why in the world does it seem like such a huge deal to me when my daughter first proposes it? I guess it's because I can't imagine starting out on a spontaneous journey after five in the afternoon, old fart that I am, especially if it involves turning around and coming right back the same night. And because I happen to be tired already, and every bone in my body is oriented towards getting home and settled after the errands of the day. God, I would *hate* to have to drive down to L.A. right now. But no one is asking me to do this. In fact, we are at one of those junctions where I sense that my opinion is not particularly relevant.

Still, I find I am uncomfortable with the plan. Aside from my personal resistance to it, there's an element of worry here too. You know: the mother thing. My daughter reminds me at this point that she is twenty-one years old.

I try to remember what that was like. I flash back to the time Helen and I drove six hours from Long Island to Oneonta purely on a whim and then back the same night, punchy and exhausted by daybreak on the Palisades Parkway heading into New York City, which is where a policeman stopped me for speeding. It was a pointless adventure, but we convinced ourselves it was evidence of our being free spirits, a couple of *carpe diem* gals who could act on an impulse, even a stupid one.

I hadn't realized that my father was planning to use the car to get to a job that morning until I pulled up and encountered him in the driveway, looking worried and bewildered. I escaped his wrath only because he had reached the point where he was relieved rather than angry to see me. I can still picture him standing there in his paint-splattered overalls, a red plaid thermos in his hand, buckets and brushes by his side, and a ladder leaning against the garage. I hope I had the sense to feel ashamed.

So, yes, there were adventures and misadventures aplenty. Sometimes I was taking care of business, other times just being a self-absorbed fool. Either way, I can see that I had an entirely different set of parameters back then. Distances seemed less daunting. Night meant bonus hours for living, and I stayed awake by choice. (Sleep? Isn't that why morning was invented?) Possibilities were endless, fear was not a factor, and no one could actually tell me what to do.

Here I must distinguish my daughter from myself and credit her for having serious goals and a vision. At her age I was still motivated mostly by immediate gratification and a desire to defer responsibility, although I hasten to add in my own defense that I came from a tragic and troubled home life and had a great deal more to run away from. Still, I imagined there was something clever and almost noble in my avoidance of workaday ruts, as though I were somehow aspiring to a higher standard for myself.

If I may speak in terms of my generation, I think we were all pretty certain we could avoid the traps our parents had walked into. Maybe we thought we were smarter than that. I swiftly transferred my loyalties to peers and boyfriends, to whom I attributed great wisdom, and I seem to have squandered staggering amounts of time doing nothing at all of value, but I was incapable of feeling any sense of urgency or even reality when it came to constructive life plans. "Youth is wasted on youth," my father always said, and I would roll my eyes. I was one of *them*.

Mission L.A.? It was easily accomplished. They even stopped at In-N-Out Burger on the way home. It was sort of an adventure, I guess, and I'm sure there was laughter and intense conversation all the way there and back, because who could be more fun and interesting than the person you are in love with in your twenties?

Who cares that it could have been avoided with better planning? So what if they left the tank empty and are still fast asleep even now? They got home safely, and my daughter's passport will be ready for her trip, and her sweet belief in the manageability of things has been nicely reaffirmed.

What I want to know is when did *I* become the person who sees all the barriers? When did I become the one you tune out, the one who warns and chides, who craves spontaneity but would just as soon stay home? When did I become the boring one who calculates costs and lies awake worrying and insists on being instructive even knowing full well that the only teacher is life itself? Youth, you see, is a foreign country. Maybe even a different planet. And I've left it far behind.

We Had Kids

"We had kids." That's what Kit said to Beverly one evening, just an old married couple driving along the ranch road, an empty house awaiting them. We all experience it sometimes, that jolting realization that we did it and it's over…and it all went by so much faster than we could have ever imagined. It was our world once, an epic experience that challenged and delighted, exhausted and exhilarated, gave shape to our days, worries to our nights, and utterly consumed us. Then, quite suddenly, they were all grown up…and here we are, remembering. We had kids.

I was thinking of it especially now because my daughter had been visiting from England and would be leaving the next day, and I was already bracing myself for the part I hate, the good-bye part. I think I've been doing pretty well with this whole business of her living so faraway, by and large respecting her autonomy, accepting that it's healthy and normal for young adults to leave the nest and have lives of their own. Really, I get it. But now that she had been with us for three weeks, I couldn't help but feel emotional about seeing her off…and then having to get used to her absence all over again.

Maybe it wouldn't be quite so tough if things had been better in my own head. It had been a strange year…an ongoing backdrop of misery pertaining to a nephew's brain injury and a sister's grief and panic, none of it "my" problem, but it weighed heavy on my heart and changed the lens through which I view the world. Meanwhile, my elderly mother had been suffering the ravages of some awful skin disease and was dispatched to a hospital. Not "my" problem either, and nothing I could do about it, but this is depressing stuff, let's face it.

Meanwhile, here in my own insular world, I was snagged on all sorts of cliché questions, like what am I doing that matters? I'm trying so hard to figure out my role... not just vis-a-vis my daughter, a presence both familiar and strange who lit here for a while...but in a larger sense. I can see so many things that I no longer am, and so many things it is too late to become, but I haven't a clue what really to do. I still feel like I'm supposed to have something very important in place, but all I can manage is to navigate day by day. And I'm quite aware that my issues and insecurities are comically luxurious—definitely First World problems—but these are my musings lately nonetheless, and I've no epiphanies in sight.

It's a funny time of life. I recently read a Martin Amis interview in which he said, "You turn sixty and there's this: 'This is going to turn out well. This can't turn out well.' But life grows in value because of your leave-taking with regard to it. Not very significant things suddenly look very poignant and charming. This particular period of my life is full of daily novelty. That turns out to be worth a great deal."

Daily novelty. I perceive it that way too. So much of it is delightful and absurd and surprising—but also, as Amis says, poignant. It's that leave-taking aspect, and I seem to be fixated on the poignancy. While my daughter was here, we went to San Francisco, meant to be a carefree time, but as we walked around that pastel city beneath glorious blue skies, I was struck by what hard lives so many lead, how fragile we all are, how quickly everything goes by. (I know. I sound like Woody Allen but without any laughs.)

Maybe I'd be fine if I could just have some peace from my family of origin and the whip-cracking of old ghosts. And maybe all these words I'm writing are nothing more than a protracted whine. We baby-ish boomers make a lot of noise. But it's not an easy thing, being human, even in a life of relative ease. Who knew how swiftly the decades would pass? Who knew that being sixty-something would feel so sudden and strange?

Who knew we would even then just be ourselves trapped in ill-fitting bodies, requiring so much adjustment and learning and grace? And all the while knowing the real decline has just begun...

Oh, I've been lucky in so many ways. I have a daughter who grew up smart and healthy and is happily on her way. I am loved and safe and well taken care of and free to indulge in all this blabbing and self-analysis. I have a handful of cherished friends. And I live in a place of beauty and wildness that continues to amaze me. Despite the kvetching, I am grateful every day.

Lately, too, there has been the gift of time with younger friends—our neighbors Ryan and Carey, for example. It still surprises me that they hang around with us, and I hope our get-togethers have been more to them than pity dates. Being older sometimes feels a little like having a mild disability that demands of others a bit of patience and tolerance. When my daughter's boyfriend was here, he jokingly said something about spending time with old people, and Carey quipped that there weren't a lot of choices in these parts, and I felt momentarily crushed until I realized that this *is* one of the beautiful things about living in our odd little community: friendships do form across generations. They are based on shared values and interests, geographical proximity, and some hard to define kindred-ness of spirit. It's true we old farts have a longer view, a different sense of time that youth can never fully grasp, but age does not entirely define us. If someone can see the original person trapped inside the decrepit container, well, the gap in ages ceases to matter.

Oh, it matters some. But here we are. It was a weekend of old friends, new friends, apricot pie, daughter reading in the big red armchair, full moon, wind-rattled windows, and a suitcase downstairs waiting to be packed. Tomorrow would bring the parting part, and that familiar ache that isn't really sadness 'cause it's just the way things are. I already knew how it would all unfold: a morning drive to the airport bus, then returning to a vacancy we'll fill with other things. We'll touch base, stay busy, seek the meaning and the joy, and feel time rushing past. There will always be a void but we avoid peering into it.

And now and then it hits us: We had kids.

Flailing

I can picture my daughter now, riding her bike to see us at the little St. Clements apartment we rented for our visit. Her thick dark hair is pulled back and a magenta scarf sets off her pale and luminous skin, and I think, though I am certainly not objective, that she is beautiful. But there's something fierce about her too. She says what she thinks and isn't gentle with me.

And I try too hard. It's a far and extravagant journey we have taken just to see her, and there's a lot of accumulated curiosity and yearning and love to be expressed and fulfilled in a short space of time. It puts pressure on us; I realize that.

She's busy. She has just started a PhD program and she's excited about it, but it's demanding. She carries a heavy bag over her shoulders, and in every spare moment, she pulls out a book, or an article, or her laptop, and I see her reading and taking notes with that familiar intensity she has demonstrated since childhood. I don't dare interrupt. And she's worried about money, of which she has almost none. Also, she just finished writing a book, which will be out before Christmas, a pretty impressive accomplishment, but not without its strains and stresses.

And we're planning a trip, a quick, easy dash to Berlin, which is lovely and worthwhile, but of course doesn't turn out to be particularly quick or easy, and actually amps up the pressure even more. (Travel is stressful…had you noticed?)

And she's young, and facing all the usual questions and challenges that arise, all the insecurities and uncertainties of youth, all the issues of decision and destiny that seem to beg for immediate answers even while such answers are impossible. I think she thinks I wouldn't understand.

As for me, I am very much *not* young. And what pressures I feel are certainly real to me but perhaps to others abstract and luxurious. I am looking here at my life's last good season, trying to make meaning and avert the sense of bitterness and regret that seems easy for older people to fall into. I don't want to be so focused on the train that left the station that I fail to notice how lovely is the town I'm left behind in.

Oh, I can see that I am silly at times, good for a laugh but near enough to my expiration date to veer towards pathetic. And I can see how I am a little like the idle rich but without the money, and disturbingly Prufrock-ian. I can even see how someone might lose patience with me. Why don't I just write, or take a class, or volunteer, or start a full-fledged garden? Why don't I just savor the present and make that my art?

Partly because I'm haunted and it bogs me down. Here's an example: just recently I overheard a woman talking about her recovery from kidney donor surgery, and I was shocked by the unexpected surge of nausea I felt as painful memories rushed over me. Two siblings with kidney disease, their lives cruelly abbreviated, and here I am with two kidneys, browsing in a shop in Santa Barbara. It's classic survivor guilt. Get over it.

But we all have our burdens, and all of us suffer. That much I have learned. I guess the trick is to keep the suffering from spreading like a cancer, negating even the beautiful things, which is not an easy task. While I was looking at rainbows in the highlands of Scotland, a Pakistani girl was shot for going to school. I don't know how to reconcile the different realities. The world is fraught with incongruous and incompatible facts.

Mr. Harbor, my daughter's boyfriend's ninety-two-year-old grandfather, says he doesn't know what he believes, really, even now. We have gathered in Oxford for dinner on a rainy evening, and the conversation includes silly British and American banter on the correct pronunciation of saws, source, sores, sauce, and sausage, but Mr. Harbor is recently widowed and palpably sad. He's heard that we're planning a trip to the Lake District, a place that holds fond memories for him, and he's brought a map and two old books with black and white photographs of mountain paths, grazing sheep, stone bridges and cottages, and he points out roads he cycled as a boy with his father. He looks down at the map with deep concentration and perhaps for a moment is a young man again, cresting a hill, descending into green, everything still in front of him. He sighs.

"I know it isn't easy," I tell him, in a well-intentioned if lame attempt at sympathy.

"It surely isn't," he says. He looks dapper in his suit and vest and is far too gracious to mock me, but I am beginning to know that I don't really know.

And yet, when a shadow of remorse falls visibly over him, I want to touch his hand and tell him to be gentle with himself. For even without having known him very long, I am certain he did the best he could with whatever he was given, and it cannot have been easy, because life never is. But isn't it also wonderful?

Maybe I want to tell my daughter something like that, too. But it always comes out wrong, ill timed, too emotional, or worse...kind of goofy and inappropriate. "Inappropriate" is a word she has applied to me more than once.

But she's helping me to see myself more objectively. For example, I zigzag when I walk. This is because I notice things all over the place and bounce around like a pinball, swerving erratically and unpredictably, which is good to know because it makes it hard for people who want to walk with me, and it might even be a metaphor for how I approach my life.

And speaking of noticing things, I apparently report on oddities and wonders that are not odd or wondrous at all. "Mom," she tells me, "I know you've traveled and done a lot of things, but I don't think you realize what a rare world you live in now. It's a very small world, and there's nothing typical about it, and a lot of the stuff that surprises you when you step outside is really not that unusual."

Here's something I find extraordinary. My daughter swims. More than that, she swims regularly, and it's become essential to her. Even in Berlin, she ventured out with swimsuit, cap, and goggles to do laps in pools in vintage pre-war buildings. And I cannot say for sure, but I imagine it is how she renews herself, emerging calmer and quieter, tired but also strong and self-contained. It's her own sacred time.

Maybe that, too, is an ordinary thing, but it amazes me, and it makes me proud. I never did learn to swim. I never learned so many things that my daughter does and does well. And this belongs to *her*...I realize that...but maybe it's indicative too of something I did right, even if accidentally.

What is it that I want from her? I don't even know, but I try too hard to get it. I suppose I want some tenderness, some acknowledgement, some love expressed. But these are implicit, and trying to tear them out into the open as I do is...well, maybe inappropriate? I embarrass her. I say things that needn't be said and expect her to do the same.

On a particularly rushed and harrowed travel day, at the airport in Berlin, she snaps at me. I don't even remember the details, but she blames me for something, most unfairly, and I feel wronged and hurt. A door inside of me clicks shut and I decide that from this point on, I will remain cool and reserved with her. I sit beside her on a bench beneath the clock and the board of arrivals and departures and say nothing. I won't go back for more abuse. Ever.

"I'm sorry, Mom," she says, and it's like magic how I melt. "I get stressed. It's not your fault."

Oh my God. Not my fault. Not my fault. My heart opens up and fills to the brim with gratitude and all of it wants to spill out, but I just say, "It's okay." I don't even add how much I love her, because she probably knows, and I sense that this is one of those situations where I should just tread lightly and not take it over the top. I contain myself.

A few days later, back in Oxford, I take her out to buy her new shoes, which she desperately needs. It's such a mother-daughter thing, and I am giddy with it. But within minutes it is clear that this is a necessary errand to her, not a leisurely outing. She's conspicuously irritated by everything and eager to get back to the library, and there's a spark in her that would be all too easy to ignite. So I try to rise above it. I try to be as a mother should be:

patient, calm, understanding. I try my hand at dignity and restraint, and I don't take her annoyance personally because it suddenly seems clear that she is worried and hurried and it has nothing to do with me. I focus on how bravely she is taking on new challenges, how daunting it must seem, how spirited she is. I remember that she is twenty-five years old. And oh, the joy I feel when I see her in her new shoes! It's a goofy, silly, irrational kind of joy, but it's joy nonetheless. I wisely keep it to myself.

That evening during dinner, I mention to her how much I wish that I could dance, but dancing is another thing I never learned to do. "I just don't know how to move," I say. "I wouldn't even know what to do with my hands."

She looks at me in an almost maternal way. "Mom," she says, "just get out there and flail. You certainly know how to flail."

And I do. I've been flailing for years, and will likely continue.

Thorns And Roses

"Your father was quite the charmer," said the lady in my dream. Her powdered face looked at least eight decades old, her dyed reddish hair was curly and short. She was a brassy sort, but good-natured, and she managed the building of the apartment into which, in my dream, I had wandered. It was a little flat in Brooklyn with yellow-hued walls and green tiles and shiny linoleum, a clean, uncluttered place, an apartment with good bones. "Oh, vintage linoleum!" I said stupidly, and I was vaguely aware of having stepped into the best of the 1950s, the era of my childhood.

More important, I had discovered my father's secret refuge in the city, and even in his absence there was evidence of him: the graceful remnants of a hand-painted mural in a foyer, the gleaming floors, the tidiness...it made me so happy to know that there had been a place of retreat for him, a place where he could be himself, accountable to no one, unburdened and autonomous.

"It's still his," said the lady, "or yours, if you want it." I wanted it. I did.

So it was what I call a good dream, a wish fulfilled retroactively, a sense of the presence of someone I loved. I guess the wish is that my father had had more happiness, a sweet hidden life apart from the struggles that I witnessed. But isn't it ridiculous the degree to which he still inhabits my head? It reminds me of a cartoon I read in The New Yorker, where a mother is tucking in her little boy and reassuring him: "The only ghosts you need fear are the ghosts of your past–which will gnaw away at your soul, riddle you with self-doubt, and ultimately sap you of your will to live." That pretty much sums it up, although it hasn't quite sapped me of the will to live.

In fact, another telling aspect of the dream is how much I coveted that apartment for myself, a little getaway flat like my friend Cornelia has in Berlin, but in a Brooklyn that no longer exists. How easily I could picture the neighborhood in summer rain, everything I need nearby, and myself by a window and the warm-hued wall, leaning back easily into occasional solitudes that bear no resemblance to loneliness, feeling safe and certain in a place that fits me like a nest.

> *Someone who goes with half a loaf of bread*
> *to a small place that fits like a nest around him,*
> *someone who wants no more, who's not himself*
> *longed for by anyone else,*
> *He is a letter to everyone. You open it.*
> *It says, Live.*

That's from Rumi, translated by John Moyne and Coleman Barks, and I don't know exactly why, but this seemed the time to share it.

Maybe it's because last week I heard a catch in my sister's voice and understood that she dwells on the constant cusp of tears, and the catch was like a door unlatching, but I stepped back before it opened. And I was with a friend when she crashed her bicycle, over the handlebars, onto the gravel like a crumpled flower, tumbling in an instant from fresh and carefree to bruised and askew, and I remembered again how fragile we are. And I found a bookshop tucked away like a secret temple in an old Santa Barbara adobe, crammed with rare books and prints and antiquities, with an Oxford sort of ambiance, dark wood, a slant of light, the smell of aging pages. There was a conversation with a Japanese man who had been pulled from his life and placed in an internment camp in 1941 but chose to harvest kindness from his history. And there was an afternoon in the living room when Monte was listening to the nimble, husky guitar of Junior Brown and he suddenly said, "Let's waltz" and took my hand, and waltz we did.

So I'm looking up, climbing out of a dark place, refueling my light. My friend Dan suggested a book by Jack Kornfield in which I promptly found this passage: "When Siddhartha sat by the river at the end of the story by Herman Hesse that many of us read in high school, he finally learned to listen. He realized that all the many voices in the river comprise the music of life: the good and evil, the pleasures and the sorrows, the grief and the laughter, the yearnings and the love. His spirit was no longer in contention with all of life. He found that along with the struggles was also an unshakable joy."

Rumi again:

When you go to a garden,
do you look at thorns or flowers?
Spend more time with roses and jasmine.

The thorns will make themselves known. Remember roses, jasmine, or even a clumsy waltz.

Going Back To Brooklyn

This particular day was a holiday, but the streets were already peopled with dog-walkers, joggers, and baby stroller pushers. I tried to imagine what it would be like to live in this leafy neighborhood, with its old brownstone houses and cobblestone streets, but my Brooklyn roots are shabbier, and my original street, Coney Island Avenue, is a long way from gentrification. However, despite my warnings that there wouldn't be much to see, my dear friend Vickie wanted to see my childhood home, and we set out on the Number 5 train, transferring to the Q and getting off at Beverley Road.

Beverley Road is one of the oldest of the MTA stations, built as an actual station, with wooden benches, a ticket office, and classy mosaic lettering and borders. I vividly remember getting on and off this stop with my mother when I was a little girl, seeing the bridge across the tracks, a house where violets grew along a fence, and of course the steep steps up to the street that were shielded like a greenhouse by glass windows. Vickie and I were about to walk out into western Flatbush and one of Brooklyn's loveliest neighborhoods, now a designated historical district known as Ditmas Park. Its shady streets are lined with houses from Victorian times, many with porches and beautiful landscaping. Some were now in disrepair or need of paint, but I wandered these streets often in the 1950s choosing the houses I would love to live in and maybe would someday.

We were now blocks away but a world apart from Coney Island Avenue. The route of fifty years ago kicked in again: turn left and walk straight. There was the border of zigzagged bricks Carol and I always had to jump along, there was the stately house from whose upper windows an enviable young girl once looked out at me, there was the great front porch I would have liked to sit upon, still shaded by tall trees. As we approached Coney Island Avenue, the houses gave way to a stretch of stores. I saw where Anthony's salon had been, where my sisters and I got our hair de-tangled and cut, and where Dave's newsstand had stood, where we always got yelled at for reading...never buying...the comic books, learning to scan quickly before crabby Dave noticed and told us to scram. We reached the corner. "There's my block," I announced to Vickie.

Coney Island Avenue is a wide and busy thoroughfare that traverses Brooklyn from Prospect Park to Coney Island. We crossed over to the side I lived on, turned left, and I began reciting, as though in a trance, the tedious significance of each doorway. That's where the Keatings lived, and that's where Mr. Blitstein's lumber yard was, and there's my best friend Carol Bessey's house, and there was the Miliccis' house, and the Wittners next door to us, and there's where Mrs. Johnson was crossing the street when she got hit by a car. There's the stoop, and there's where we played jump rope, and there's where we bounced a pink *Spaldeen* ball against a wall, and there on the other side of the street, beyond the Mobil gas station, is where we paid the rent to Mr. Molinari, forty bucks a month...

At 624, my old address, we saw Scottie, an African-American man who now owns the building and has run an antique store downstairs for thirty-five years. I have come back to visit on two other occasions and thus met Scottie already. "Oh, I know who you are," he said, when I introduced myself. "How are things in California?" I guess from his perspective, every five or ten years a couple of effusive middle-aged white women come by to stare at his building as though it were a historical landmark. He's pretty cool about it, though.

We talked about the changes the neighborhood has undergone, the different ethnic and religious groups that have moved in and seem to coexist just fine, a bit of welcome tree-planting that's been happening, and a beautiful old orchard hidden behind one of the houses across the street. We ritualistically reviewed the floor plan of his apartment above, once mine: yes, that little room in back, the way you walk into the kitchen with the window overlooking the clothesline, the fire escape, and the alley below, the living room, the middle room, and the front room facing the street. I kept wishing he would at least unlock the front door so I could see the pattern of the tiles and the old wooden staircase, but he was understandably private about his domain. He did, however, lead us through his store so we could look out into the back alley for a moment, and even that had a certain charm. It's hard to explain, but to a city kid, the secret little spaces off the main street are special, somehow, the places where trees and weeds are growing, where forgotten things pile up.

"Been meaning to ask you," said Scottie, as though he'd been pondering it for several years. "Anything strange ever happen in this place? Anything mysterious?"

Sorrowful, tragic, violent, chaotic...all of that, yes. Strange and mysterious? Well, nothing beyond the weirdness and puzzle of life as it is. I shrugged.

"It's nothing too dramatic," he went on, "just a light goin' on and off for no reason, footsteps, a feeling...I got to thinking maybe something had happened here a long time ago. That kinda thing. Didn't the lady in the upstairs apartment get hit by a car? Maybe she comes back."

"Maybe so," I said, although for the life of me, I couldn't imagine any reason for Mrs. Johnson to come back. "But every old house is filled with stories. I think sometimes you can sense them."

"Yeah, we're all a part of something," said Scottie. He seemed to be in a philosophical mood, or maybe he was picking up on my wistfulness. "Here in this neighborhood we got people from all over, and we're getting along, we're doing our best. See all that stuff back there in this store? That's just stuff, a whole lotta stuff...none of it really matters. All we really got is each other, you know? And we're part of something bigger."

We said our good-byes and Vickie and I walked to the corner at Avenue C. There where Harry's grocery store and Joe's candy shop once were, another little girl with a pink scooter and a big yellow ball was having her childhood. I decided I might as well show Vickie my route to school, a ten-minute walk along Avenue C and past Ocean Parkway almost to McDonald Avenue. Vickie looked up at the somber brick building that was my school and almost shuddered. "Did you feel welcome there?" she asked.

"No, I just felt required to be there. No questions asked. I knew what was expected of me. No one was too concerned with our self-esteem in those days."

At McDonald and Church, I tried to locate the site of my grandfather's pizzeria, where I sometimes went for lunch, but nothing even vaguely resembled it. We ate in a falafel place where a man urged us to try the hot sauce. "It *says* hot, but it isn't very hot," he kept telling us, and when we finally tried it, we had to admit he was right. "You see?" he said. "You have to try everything in life!"

As Vickie and I descended into the Church Avenue subway station I remembered the teenage boys with their greaser hair and tight jeans who used to stand there singing doo-wop where the echo was good. We rode a couple of stops and got off by the park, and Vickie patiently waited as I took pictures of fire escapes, cellar doors, the curved arms of an old-style bench. Everything seemed amazing to me, like strands of old dreams coalescing into tangible objects, providing evidence that my history happened.

But it was also sad, like returning to an abandoned set long after the play has ended. Wasn't it absurd and self-indulgent to be making such a fuss over all these ancient details, these places long since occupied and transformed by the millions of souls who came after? Honestly, who takes pictures of cellar doors and benches? Why do I think any of this is important? Why am I writing about it now?

And on some level I realize it's not important at all. But do any of us ever get over our childhoods? I actually asked the question out loud. "First we understand," said Vickie. "Next we forgive. Then we're done with it."

I think Scottie's right: we're part of something bigger.

The Body's Natural Tendency

I was walking at the beach with my friend Linette. The day had the aura of a silvery dream, the air damp and salty, and a fog-thickened sky blurred the edges of things. Three or four guys were out there surfing, among them local ranch kids Nole and Andrew, and it was fun to watch them in all their exuberance and athleticism. Linette has the sea in her story and her soul, and I was happy she could be here. Her father, Henry Lum, was a surfer in Hawaii during the 1950s, a Makaha regular, the "skinny Chinaman" who rode twenty-foot waves but could barely manage a dog paddle.

"He honestly didn't know how to swim," said Linette, "but he read in a book that the body has a natural tendency to float, and he took it on faith."

Silly me. I have always assumed that swimming would be a prerequisite to surfing. But folks are forever stretching the boundaries of what you thought possible. I've been wondering lately what it would feel like to be out there, and I watch with a new kind of wistfulness.

"It was like a magic carpet ride from the very first," my neighbor Andy Neumann once said. When it comes to surfing, Andy, a certified legend, knows whereof he speaks.

"Well, that sounds pretty nice," said Linette when I told her this, "but for me it was more like being a dish rag caught in the spin cycle."

Evidently she wasn't ready that first time. But she learned; she learned so well that she even went on to instruct others. "Don't worry," she would tell them. "The body has a natural tendency to float."

Linette and I often share family stories. She's convinced that despite my being Italian and Jewish, or maybe because of it, I had a very Chinese upbringing, which might explain why we understand each other so well and laugh so much at our own foibles when we're together. There's a similarity in the guilt thing, in goals thrust upon you whether you like 'em or not, personal desires that could never acquire parental endorsement, and that brave historic moment when you make the break, defy the rules, become yourself. But of course you never really get away. It's all in your head and your heart forever. When everything is said and done, we are dutiful Chinese daughters.

And I think we're both missing our fathers today. It's an old fact for me, more recent for Linette, but I remember how it goes. In time you find yourself looking for them in the places that they loved, or you discover them anew in the ways they are remembered by people who knew them apart from you, or you glimpse them in some aspects of yourself.

Now Nole comes in and shows us a wooden surfboard he shaped and built with seven dollars' worth of wood. It's heavy and primitive, a virtual plank, but lovely in its simplicity, and it's hard to ride but he does okay. I tell him that Linette's father was riding wooden boards back in the 1950s, and riding them on giant waves. Henry Lum? No, Nole hasn't heard of him. But guys like Woody Brown knew him, and Jock Sutherland. And ol' Ray Kunze, bless his soul, who used to surf right here, he sure was impressed when he heard the name of Henry Lum.

Linette and I walk on, laughing so hard at times that I wonder why we don't hang out on a regular basis, and maybe that's what we ought to do from now on. Some people are just good for you, and Linette has the right kind of spirit.

There's good luck at the mailbox, too: a letter from another friend, an old one I'd lost touch with in recent years. Her letter explains how unexpected currents swept her away and uncharted seas engulfed her. She has made it to the shore, she says, but she came back changed forever. "I've learned that the only moment is now," she has written, "and I take more time to enjoy the little things, for I have realized they are the big things."

Back at the house water comes with the turn of a spigot and an avocado in a bowl has ripened to buttery perfection and the fog has dispersed and the room is filled with sunlight and Linette says maybe someday she can teach me how to swim and I know that this will never happen, but I feel a sense of levity and lightness so pure and inexplicable that I think it must be true: the body's natural tendency is to float.

Good-Bye To All That

Sometimes the air is still and the sea is the gold of the sandstone cliffs it mirrors in morning's honeyed sunlight. The train appears, all whistle and bluster, and clatters by noisily, an extended exclamation, then leaves a deeper silence in its wake. I walk to the junction of the main road and reflexively open the mailbox, but of course it is empty of letters, and I smile at how hope always trumps experience.

If there is a snakeskin snagged in the coyote brush, I will stoop down for a closer look; I will see that it is dry, translucent, and parchment light, a custom encasement vacated by its occupant, and I will ponder the meticulous design of its ridges and scales. I may even perceive it as beautiful, for I am learning to appreciate such things, their inviolable integrity and otherness. Then reverting to the dysfunctional home base that is my own ego, I will wistfully think about shedding and change, the many shells that have contained me, the selves that I have been, what I may yet become, and what remains.

I was a middle school teacher. My life was populated by kids aged ten to fourteen, humans who could not traverse a field without running, skipping, or inventing games that involved wrestling, dance steps, or some innovative form of tag and pursuit. I inhabited a world in which shoes appeared on rooftops, rain-slicked wooden decks were meant for sliding, and girls tap-danced side by side on a giant playground chessboard. Children smiled at me with multi-colored braces on their teeth and left drawings on my whiteboard. They told me secrets sometimes that I have never revealed and by eighth grade they forgot that I existed. They read books in a window seat, crawled under a table to write tales of runaway horses and fantasy battles, and asked questions that I could not always answer.

How many people get to try walking on coffee can stilts in the course of their workday or have their hair elaborately braided by a seventh grade girl? I did. I saw snow angels in the mountains and sand angels at the beach. I supervised the mummification of chili peppers, helped bury and excavate bogus ancient artifacts, and assisted in the placement of the planets. I was drawn into a spontaneous conga line once after a sparkling etiquette dinner in a make-believe restaurant, and I walked in silence with sixty-six kids on September 11th.

We pored over atlases with their pastel colored maps and discussed the reasons given for a war. We looked at the faces of faraway children and tried to make life better for one. We wrote thank you letters, shared stories, and interviewed our elders. We surfed the *Metro* of Washington, D.C. and hopped a cable car in San Francisco. We found poems in odd places and shining epiphanies. Once we had an all-girls' sleepover on campus, ran through the sprinklers in the dark, and fell asleep watching *Anne of Green Gables*.

Not every day was an adventure, of course, and whether adult or student, each of us endures our share of tedium and routine. But it helps to have colleagues who discuss the red-plumed grass growing by the railroad tracks, seldom heard songs of Nina Simone, fourth power polynomials, the life of poetry, whether ideas can exist without language, and the moral components of religious belief. It helps to have people who tolerate your many eccentricities and simply laugh when you remind them for the third time to turn off the coffee maker and lock the door when they leave, who listen to your troubles during a quick stop in the office and help you put them all into perspective.

Even my commute to work was wondrous. I loved the way the fog danced with the early sun as I crested the hill and descended into the valley. One morning, just south of the Pork Palace, I saw a rainbow in the fog; it was more silvery than a regular rainbow, its colors hushed and frosted. I didn't have a camera but I had to tell someone. Treebeard was standing outside during recess that day cocking his head and watching a biplane dipping and playing in the sky toward the mountains, so I told him about the rainbow. "Fogbow," he said, more verbose than usual. That night I found an entire website on fogbows, complete with photographs. They looked like haloes of light, white rainbows. "At the center," the text said, "one will find a glory."

I liked working in a place where fogbows were understood. Where kids said, "Let's get high" and meant they wanted to swing really hard on the swings. Where someone on the staff, when asked, "What's the policy on tree climbing?" responded, in all seriousness, "I think it's a good idea."

I liked getting emails from kids, and wearing costumes, and discussing books while speaking in fake accents. I liked riding my bike with the eighth grade boys, time traveling through our journals, taping cool words on the wall, making paper cranes and embroidering jeans, seeing guitars in the bathtub and kites in the sky, watching our prayer flags dissolving in threads as our beautiful hopes diffused into the universe.

I *was* a middle school teacher, and it's time to get used to that past tense. For many years I lived by the rhythms of the academic year and the ebb and flow of its cycle; I experienced the incongruous tugging of June remorse, the familiar sense of loss as I waved from the shore to people I had grown to love. It's all the more poignant when you know you're not returning.

It's a little scary, too. I am afraid of a blank fall, afraid of the quiet, afraid of becoming irrelevant. There's a lone boxcar waiting on the track today. A covey of quail bursts abruptly from the brush like questions in quick need of answer. The world seems laden with mystery and meaning—best to walk straight in with a grateful heart. At the center one will find a glory.

Picnic At Little Drake's

For whatever we lose(like a you or a me)
it's always ourselves we find in the sea

E.E. Cummings

The day was a kiln, and the ground a hard clay platter, and everyone moved slowly if they moved at all, but we had a plan in place. We would pack a makeshift picnic and go down to the beach with friends in the late afternoon, and we could walk by the shore or go for a swim or just find a spot to sit and talk, and we would stay there until dusk, or as long as we wanted.

It was a simple plan and it came to pass. Ol' Treebeard grabbed his camera and tripod and immediately went off for a solitary walk, looking at the estuary that washes out from the canyon, watching the waves, squinting at sea life with an intentness and curiosity I remembered fondly from the days when we were teachers together. Others went blissfully swimming or splashed around in the surf. A breeze came up, and distinctive currents of coolness rushed through the air, as refreshing as rivers. Sometimes you could take two steps over and suddenly find yourself in a little patch of cool air and park yourself there for a moment. On the bluff above the beach, a black bull stood unsettlingly close to the edge. To the west, towards Point Conception, the sky began its sequence of dusky pink and orange, intensified by the haze of distant fires.

I placed a bright blue cloth on a weathered redwood table and we began to unpack our repast. There were bottles of Gewürztraminer, spicy and chilled, and cold cans of Bud, and for juvenile palates like mine, some sort of sweet fruit soda. There were deviled eggs and garlic-studded pork loin, chips and dips from Trader Joe's, mushroom turnovers, slices of honeydew. "Does anyone have any interest in locks?" asked Julie. *Locks?* I thought. Doors, yes, windows, yes, but locks? And of course she pulled out a chunk of salted salmon, lox that she had prepared herself, and we proceeded to eat, appetites unbolted, doors ajar, conversation humming, a sense of well-being.

There was talk of brown bears eating nectarines and berries, of an oak forest reclaiming a certain apple orchard, of an Indian cave in the mountains. Kit and Beverly came by, fleeing the heat of the backcountry, with their laptop and a movie in their car. We talked of school days and paradigm shifts, retirement and disability, the places we'd like to travel to and the pleasures of being right here. We were a ragtag group, graying and balding, broken and repaired but not quite good as new. We were people past our prime, retired or tired, still trying to figure things out, still capable of being surprised.

Suddenly there was a shout from Julie. She had heard some sort of rattling sound coming from the front of her truck and thought there was a snake inside. Everyone approached the vehicle, some armed with sticks, prepared to gingerly poke around.

A closer look revealed the origin of the sound: a dragonfly caught inside the headlight. Monte reached in and helped the creature to extricate itself, and it shot into the air, magnificently bursting forth, erupting into freedom, and we all looked up with a-h-h-s and awe, and now we saw there was a second dragonfly that seemed to have been hovering and waiting, and the two of them sailed off together. We stood in silence for a long moment.

Then we settled down again to watch the sunset and the water's shine and the beginning of the night. Jupiter rose brightly and the broken bowl moon shattered into pieces of light that floated on the sea.

Snow On Distant Mountains

We climbed onto the sandstone ridge that juts like a backbone from the hillside above Cuarta Canyon. We peered, curious, into wind-carved caves and cupboards and seated ourselves on the rocks around a small basin filled with new rain. Looking east we saw the San Rafael Mountains covered in snow, and to the west, the gleam of sea. I pulled some sweet spirals of cinnamon rolls from my pack, a little dry and flat, but when broken and shared among four women, communion.

Later, as we gathered ourselves together to leave, Margaret stood and lingered for a moment on the far side of the pool, silhouetted against the sky. She wore an oversized navy blue rain jacket to keep out the wind; she put up the hood and wrapped her scarf more snugly around her neck, then smiled sadly, looking small and brave. She was three weeks into widowhood. "I face my fate," she said.

Margaret and I grew close in these days after her husband's death. She still calls me her little sister sometimes, even though I am bigger than she is. She's Chinese, and she often apologizes for her English, which is far better than she thinks, and she is a shy person, an observer. Even as a child, she remembers feeling incomplete, out of kilter, sensing the presence of something unseen and yearning to know it. The universe is limitless, she told me once, and if we do not see something or understand it, that doesn't mean it isn't there. She is trying to find strength now in these thoughts. "I'm still here," she says. "There has to be a reason."

A day or two after our hike to the ridge I decided to visit Margaret and see how she was doing. I rode my bike up the muddy, rutted road of Sacate Canyon, splashed my way across two streams, and climbed the long steep hill to her house. I rapped at every door and called her name, and when she emerged, she was so visibly pleased to see me, my own heart lifted. "Let me cook for you," she said. I guess we all crave a welcome like that.

"I show you how I cook Chinese noodles," she said, emptying a package into a steaming pot, stir-frying strips of pork lightly dusted with cornstarch, adding shitake mushrooms, and chopped up cabbage...and soy sauce, not just any brand, but a special kind from the Chinese market in L.A. She set out two bowls for us, and we sat at the table in front of the window. We looked out onto the Channel Islands, the rise and dip of greening hills, and a lone horse by the barn.

She told me that the power had gone out during the storm the night before. All the windows shuddered, and loose things banged about, and she'd lain awake in the dark, feeling lost at sea, then rose at daybreak's first gray light, made tea, and fed the cat. She thought about the brief happy season she and her husband had enjoyed together in this house.

"But my journey is not done," she said, even if she sometimes wishes it were. She needs to get her bearings, fathom the hollow of loss, grasp a new reality.

And I am company today. It's all I have to offer. So Margaret and I sit side-by-side, facing the window, eating Chinese noodles, and there's snow on distant mountains. Who can say what disparate geographies may somehow connect? Who knows what great upheavals will tumble souls together? Who could have ever imagined how far from where we started we'd find home?

On the table is a book Margaret is reading. I open it at random and see vertical columns of Chinese characters lined up like tapestries upon each page. She shows me the beginning at the end of the book.

The Egg Woman

Clamor of questions,
You clamor of answers,
Here's your egg.

C.G. Hanzlicek

Jeanne lives in a little house up the canyon with a driveway so steep your calves start to ache before you've reached the top. I can hear her chickens whenever I go by, and sometimes their crowing and squawking carries on the wind into my own backyard. It's a lunatic sound, and I love it. Jeanne started with seven chickens but inherited more, and they have multiplied tenfold. They are all hens, except for Elvis, Wayne, and Romero, three stereotypically cocky roosters certain of their place in life. I see them strutting around ridiculously in their outlandish feathers, and I cannot help but laugh at the sight. Jeanne's house, which has always been the scene of impressive one-woman industry, has thus also become a madcap zone where clucks and chuckles hang in the air, punctuated by sporadic rooster screams. There is something about chickens that makes me not take myself so seriously.

Jeanne sees the humor of them too, but mostly she sees the eggs. "What a beautiful, perfect creation," she will say, cupping one carefully in her hand, or marveling at the size and smoothness of another. "A miraculous thing. Sustenance in a shell." She has set up a sign and an honor box just outside the gate to her property, and for five dollars a dozen, neighbors can buy fresh eggs. They are superior eggs…the flavor fresher, the yolks more yellow. They are somehow the essence of egg, and this is a good thing, even if you didn't know you had been missing it.

It's a lot of work, keeping this egg operation going. One summer Jeanne designed a large and comfortable chicken apartment so the girls, as she calls them, could settle more safely and comfortably at night. Two days after it was finished, the infamous Gaviota winds kicked up, and an old oak tree weakened at the core by fire fifty years earlier finally snapped and crashed directly onto the brand new coop. The coop was smashed beyond repair, and a couple of hens were crushed, and Jeanne took a deep breath, cleared up the mess, and rebuilt a little further from the trees. "Chicken Little was right that time," she said.

That's the way it is around here. There are weeds to whack and brush to clear, fallen trees to be removed, everything demanding maintenance and tending. Water needs pumping, fence is broken, the phone line unreliable. Rodents occupy the hidden crannies of dwellings and car engines, and there's so much dust—the outside is forever getting in. Rural life is a work always in progress and a labor of love.

But then there is the wonder. Sometimes I see Jeanne working in her garden and we shout across the creek the way housewives used to shout over backyard fences as they hung their laundry on the line with wooden clothespins, except that we'll be talking about secret chanterelles, or wild strawberries on the ridge, about tides turning, hens laying, and last night's orange moon. She tells me that she glimpsed the bear that's been eating the apricots, and that her brand new chickens, hatched in Iowa, are now ensconced in their California digs. A few feathery girls wander by, Romero crows, and I wedge a carton of eggs into my backpack and carefully pedal home.

Navigation Tools

My beautiful mother-in-law, a role model of class and intelligence in her eighties, made an interesting observation about my generation once: we face each life passage with such angst and noise you'd think no one else had ever before gone through it. It's true we boomers talk a lot. I suppose that's because there are so many of us…and we only recently realized we're not young anymore and need to discuss that with all the fervor it warrants. As my friend Vickie says, we won't go gently.

In this spirit of amazed navel gazing and earnest searching for significance, I decided when I turned sixty to list a few insights and tips I had thus far accrued—a set of navigation tools, if you will. Some are obvious and some are mere opinion, and I admit I don't always live up to the noble ones, but I'm forever striving, and I guess they're good reminders. So feel free to stash 'em with the maps and notes in your own mental glove compartment, and by all means, add and revise as you like:

1. Do not expect resolution. Questions continue and ambiguity persists. Get used to it. And the old ghosts never go away; you may as well make a space for them—just don't let 'em take over.

2. Everyone is going through something hard. Err on the side of kindness.

3. But it's okay to have boundaries. (That one still feels new to me.)

4. If you can't seem to get going on your real work, clear your desk. Or get up and do the laundry. Or sort out your closet and give lots of things away. Or pull a few weeds.

5. There is no greater skill than compromise, and even the greatest romances and adventures ultimately depend on it.

6. But a fundamental part of your being must be sacrosanct. As William Stafford said, "There is a thread you follow...you never let go of the thread." Recognize it. You cannot thrive in a situation that requires you to let go of your thread.

7. The giddiness and excitement of new love is wonderful, but nothing compares to the deep bond of shared history that develops over a long relationship. Don't ever undervalue that.

8. There is no substitute for a handwritten letter, even if it's just a short note, the kind with a stamp and a postmark that arrives in the mail. To facilitate this, own at least one good pen that you like the feel of. Know where it is.

9. While we're on the subject of writing: always carry pencil and paper. Those fragments and epiphanies that occur to you while you're outside walking or riding your bike will otherwise evaporate.

10. Embrace technology. Maintain a healthy degree of informed skepticism, but try to stay up to date and figure out how to make it work for you. To be a Luddite is to become irrelevant—or even more irrelevant than you already are.

11. Going outside for a walk almost always makes you feel better. Many advocate sitting

still, but I think motion is the best therapy. If you're lucky enough to have the capability, get moving.

12. Which reminds me: in the ongoing quest for shoes that are cute as well as comfortable, comfortable always trumps cute. Seldom do they overlap.

13. Sometimes you already know the answer. Listen for it.

14. Regret is poison, so spit it out and move on, which I realize isn't easy. But note that regret is most often the result of a loving thing not done. Learn from that.

15. Forgive yourself. You too are worthy of compassion. And stop trying to please those who can never be pleased. Including dead people.

16. Inhabit your life fully. Don't dilute your experience by holding back and second-guessing your choices. Even if you are uncertain, you are more likely to figure things out by being present. Go through the motions until the real thing kicks in.

17. A huge part of happiness is simply giving yourself permission to be happy. (It's far too easy to succumb to sadness; whistling in the dark is a perfectly valid strategy.)

18. It is impossible to underestimate the degree to which insufficient sleep or exercise negatively affects your outlook.

19. Don't waste too much effort giving advice to people who are a lot younger than you. They can never fully understand you. By the very nature of their youth, they have a fundamentally different sense of time and cannot possibly grasp how swiftly everything passes, or the various ramifications of this fact...and the context in which they function isn't what we remember either. Give up the idea that you were going to have ongoing directive input into the life of your adult son or daughter.

20. Rant to your girlfriends, not your husband. Your girlfriends will commiserate. Your husband will think he has to fix it. (Husbands: sometimes we just like to vent; that doesn't mean you're responsible.)

21. Decisions based largely on fear or lack of faith in yourself don't turn out well. Remember that the best things you've ever done were often preceded by disapproval and dire warnings, and the things you're proudest of achieving were never the easiest. But don't compare yourself to others, and don't explain or apologize for not being more than you are. Sometimes simply surviving and passing as normal is a remarkable accomplishment.

22. Prospects really did narrow as you aged. The world no longer seems a vast array of possibilities from which to choose, and you might as well admit that many of your long-held hopes and ambitions have ceased to be realistic. But alternative paths would have been different, not better—remember that—and some of the old mythologies you've had to relinquish were just that: mythologies. It's late. Lighten up. There is likely some truth to those rumors of mortality.

23. Forget about the lines under your eyes and furrows in the forehead. Anyone who doesn't have these is either younger than you or spent a lot of money on repairs. If you have that kind of money, go on a trip. You'd rather *have* an experience than *be* an experience...right?

24. Life is astonishing and implausible. This very moment is absurdly unlikely. Things we cannot begin to imagine are yet to happen, and some of them will be good.

25. If you love someone, please...oh please...let them know.

Safe

It was a strange and vivid dream that I remembered clearly when I awoke. My neighbor Andy was driving me someplace in a small jeep-like vehicle. He was going very fast over rugged bluffs and downward towards the coast. Whenever we hit a bump, I was lifted from my seat; it was very much like riding a bucking bronco, not that I've ever done that. I don't know why Andy was in such a hurry—maybe the surf was really great that day— but I finally asked him to let me out and I would find my own way back. I turned in the direction of what I thought was Sacate Canyon, but when I ascended the top of the bluff and over to the other side, nothing was familiar.

In fact, the place upon which I gazed was oddly urban, and I surmised that we had been a whole lot further down the coast than I originally thought. I found my way to a junction of two wide paved roads: Hope Boulevard and Hope Avenue, which formed a triangular area called Hope Island. Well, I thought, if you are going to be lost, Hope Island is certainly a hopeful-sounding place to have landed, even if a tad cliché. My immediate strategy was to simply call Monte, ask him to find the location on Google maps, and come and get me, but since this expedition had started out as a ranch drive with Andy, I didn't have a cell phone, money, or any identification on me.

I was a nameless, penniless stranger stranded on Hope Island.

Conveniently, there was a man in pink velour sweat pants standing around selling bagels, balloons, and theater tickets. (What can I say? It was a dream.) He had access to an old-fashioned office phone, the kind with buttons that light up, and he grudgingly let me use it, but when I reached Monte (who was somehow home with our daughter, who was somehow about twelve years old again) he was unexpectedly resistant to come and rescue me. "You got yourself there," he said, "maybe you should try to figure it out."

Back in wide-awake real life a day later, Monte and I were driving to Los Angeles where he had a business meeting, and I described this dream to him. One of his duties as husband is to serve as receptacle for my mental debris; I like to know what my subconscious is trying to tell me, and he's usually quite insightful. I asked him if he had any ideas. "This is not obvious?" he said. "Andy represents your neighbors and community, your own familiar world. But you've gotten pulled away from home by the demands of the latest epic crisis, and by overwhelming problems you feel called upon to help with, and you know what? You're basically on your own there. It's a very clear dream. Heavy handed, even. You can't save those people and I can't save you. Save yourself. Draw some boundaries. Reclaim your lost identity."

He's blunt, but he makes his point.

So while Monte went to a meeting in some big building on Wilshire Boulevard, I had an hour or so to wander around Los Angeles. I randomly chose a direction, strolled a few blocks, and promptly came upon a street called...you guessed it...Hope! Talk about *déjà vu.* It was in a run-down neighborhood and seemed to culminate in a vacant area, maybe a parking lot, not much to see. I heard voices carrying from a block or two away, repetitious and sing-song. The source was a very orderly picket line with placard-carrying workers marching back and forth, chanting in unison, and I couldn't quite hear what they were saying, but the sound of it was carrying across the empty streets, bouncing against buildings, and echoing back. It was haunting and eerie...dream-like.

I wandered some more. I don't know L.A. and can't tell you exactly what neighborhood I was in, but it was someplace in the old part of downtown, and many of the buildings were shabby and in disrepair. I saw the dilapidated marquees of formerly fancy theaters, and brick facades with the faded lettering from long-ago advertising, and on one tall wall the painted message "Jesus Saves." In the distance I saw a skeletal tower rising above rooftops, resembling some Gothic ruin, and as I paused to look up at it, an African-American woman who was passing by smiled at me and said, with a tone of certainty and sincerity, "I just want you to know God loves you. Don't you worry. Have a good day."

On that very street corner there was an old lock, vault, and burglar alarm store. On one side it said "security" in big block letters, yellow on green, and there was an enormous yellow key, very reassuring, a key you'd never lose, and biggest of all, at the front entrance, was just this one emphatic word: SAFE.

I wondered, my frame of mind being as it's lately been, if all of us aren't simply looking to be saved or be safe, really, in one way or another. I thought about childhood games of chase and tag, how we would arbitrarily proclaim a certain doorway, sewer grating, or traffic light as safe, then run to it and touch it. Maybe sometimes, out of breath, we would fully lean into it, relieved and secure, sheltered in the framework of our own invented rules.

But of course we're never safe. We find ourselves in alien landscapes, wondering how we got there, yearning for what was. Sometimes the very worst things happen, to us or other people, and if it's to others the trick is knowing how much and how little we can offer. Maybe we call a time out, or claim a safe zone, or retreat within, or take a leap of faith. We polish off our compass, but it's mostly trial and error. And if hope turns out to be a vacant island, well, at least it's a place to park and get our bearings.

A Clattering Of Windows

I awoke to a clicking noise, sudden but elongated, a steady succession of shivering sound, like teeth chattering. The clicking quickened and became a rattling—high-pitched, thin, intimately near. Was there a rattlesnake in the room? Then the house began to vibrate, and the vibration became a rumbling, a rolling growl so deep that it was everywhere.

"It's a rocket," whispered Monte.

Now I remembered. The launch of some sort of weather satellite booster had been scheduled for the wee hours of this morning. Vandenberg Air Force base is about thirty miles from here, just over the mountains, and although these space age launches seem to contrast oddly with Gaviota's bucolic hills and cattle ranches, proximity to the coast and low population density render the area well-suited for the purpose. The base launched its first ballistic missile in 1958 and soon became the regular site for test firings of strategic missile weapon systems and polar-orbiting satellite launches.

Local rancher Bob Isaacson once described the surreal sight of an Atlas missile launch during a post-branding barbecue he attended at Las Cruces Ranch in the 1960s. Cowboys fell silent as the white column collapsed and spiraled in the winds, and then someone stood up and booed. "We knew things would never be the same," Bob said.

Decades later, the launches still seem somehow dissonant and incongruous, but there is also something undeniably exciting about them, and now that I'd been jolted awake, I wanted to see the rocket's fiery path in the sky. I jumped up and ran outside.

The night sky was white with clouds. The air was unexpectedly mild, and the orchard smelled green and sweet. It had been drizzling earlier, and the deck was still wet. I could see no trace of the launch, but the growling vibration continued, and everything of earth seemed to be holding its breath waiting for it to pass. As my eyes grew accustomed to the darkness, I perceived the shapes of the hills, the depth of the woods, the hush and wonder of all that was always there. The night held life within its shadows. I sensed its wildness and mystery.

The rocket became irrelevant. It seemed that I was bearing witness to a vast secret, an older kind of miracle that had been out there all along. I stood there in my bare feet listening for a long time until the shuddering of space noise receded into stillness.

I knew that something special had transpired and it stayed with me in the days that followed. I understood it when I came upon these words in an essay by Orhan Pamuk: "To sense that life is deeper than we think it is, and the world more meaningful, does a person have to wake in the middle of the night to clattering windows, to wind blowing through a gap in the curtains, and the sounds of thunder?"

Once in awhile, yes.

The Heart's Slow Learning

There are no events but thoughts and the heart's hard turning,
the heart's slow learning where to love and whom.

Annie Dillard

"Nothing matters but who loves you and how well they perform in this." My father, the first of all my teachers, wrote those words to me in a letter long ago. They seem to be the answer to a question I will ultimately ask, but at the time I read them as a reprimand. I was hiding from him then, from his sad eyes and great disappointment, from his ominous warnings and the heaviness of his own accumulated nevers and regrets. *The clock is ticking* he would say, *the clock is ticking*. But the ticking of the clock was irrelevant to me, for I was twenty-three and still immortal. Even if life was some kind of race, I figured I could enter it later and catch up.

My father lived his entire life on the East Coast except for a South American adventure in the 1930s, and his brief wartime assignment at Camp Cooke. Years later, he spoke wistfully of Santa Barbara, recalling a beauty that seemed almost mythical to him. He always wished he could return someday under different circumstances, but of course he never did. Maybe by living here now I am fulfilling his dream by proxy. I like looking at parts of the landscape that have remained unchanged, seeing what he may have seen. But try as I might, I can't really imagine him here. He'd be too happy.

A memory comes to me of a winter day I spent with him in Manhattan once. How is it that I had him to myself? There's noise and traffic, gray sky, gray buildings, marble steps, and an imposing façade, maybe a bank. He buys a small paper bag of hot steamed chestnuts from a vendor on the street and I hold the bag up close to my face and feel its warmth. I am a gap-toothed girl in a red and white striped scarf and a blue coat missing two buttons. My ears are cold, my nose is running, and there's a sense, as always, of worry and hurry. But the chestnuts beneath their hard brown skins are buttery and satisfying, and I'm here with my father, safe and loved. I wish we didn't have to go home, where this glorious day will end in a fight, where the best in him will be misunderstood, where all the turning points will take us in circles and the patterns will repeat themselves into hopelessness. I'm carrying a patent leather purse that holds a lucky green rabbit's foot. My fingers travel through the fur of the rabbit's foot, touching its tiny sharp nails.

The clock was ticking. His letters always appear to have been written in haste, his penmanship boldly abstracted, devoid of curves, clear and outspoken. Now he's been dead for thirty-five years, and I read his words, their impact unexpired, parsing his proclamations like scripture. *What matters*, he said, is not only who loves you, but *how well they perform in this*, implying measurement and accountability, and with it, the possibility of falling short. I no longer have the excuse of being young.

There is a tray of butterfly wings arranged under glass on a cabinet in my house. The wings are yellow and iridescent blue, positioned in an ornate pattern and bordered by a frame of inlaid parquetry. The young man who would become my father bought that tray in South America, carefully storing it on the ship on which he worked as a cook to pay his passage, carrying it home across the city, and setting it atop a bureau drawer in a Brooklyn railroad flat. As a girl, I stood on a stool and looked in wonderment at the luminous wings of things once living, treasured proof of a long-ago journey...and of my father's wandering spirit, secret and suppressed, and a life he had before me. Eventually the tray was stashed in the attic and forgotten. Many years later I discovered and claimed it, and I brought it here where I see it every day, its colors going gold with time and sunlight.

Now I try to find some calculus of meaning, beginning with my father's formula, factoring in loss, subtracting irrevocable mistakes, values increased by the chance of doing better. Sometimes I think I am learning too slowly; everything's spinning so fast. In the nights I listen to the clock's conspicuous ticking and the humming of the house beneath all sound.

Transition Zone

...for the world must be loved this much
if you're going to say "I lived".

Nazim Hikmet

I live in a transition zone. This is literally true: the Gaviota coast is a bioregional borderland with both northern and southern species of California plant life—sword fern and tanbark oak, summer holly and coastal sage scrub. Even if I didn't know that, I could look down at the canyon from one of the hills and clearly see the shift from black-green vegetation to the sandy earth and pale rock upon which my little house sits like a box of light. At nearby Point Conception, where the Santa Barbara Channel meets the Pacific, the east-west trending coastline bends into a south-north course, a storied corner sometimes called the Western Gate. My home is on an off-the-grid parcel of acreage at the Hollister Ranch, one of a handful of ranches still in operation in this Gaviota zone that is neither here nor there.

The earth in these parts is worked and gently trodden—its grasslands, ridges, and creek-rich soil support farms and ranches that have survived through a century of more aggressive progress elsewhere. The result is a refreshing anachronism set amidst the unrestrained development and clamor of coastal California. It's not pristine, but nature prevails: forested riparian corridors open out to wetlands and estuaries, sweet-smelling chaparral draws hummingbirds and bees, oak-lined canyons twist along like stories we yearn to remember. Long before this land figured in the dreams of Europeans, the Chumash Indians lived their lives here and knew it as a sacred part of the universe; traces remain of their paintings on the walls of hidden caves: salamanders, sun disks, a red spiral galaxy. A visitor from the distant past would recognize the shadowed faces of these hills. The wind howls its ancient secrets through the Gaviota Pass, and we walk the wild shores that skirt the entrance to heaven.

I still wake up surprised to have found my way to such a place. But my husband's family had purchased a parcel of land in the 1970s when the Hollister Ranch was first subdivided and sold, and we visited often. We decided we would one day live there, a fantasy that needed time but was never in doubt. Eventually we managed to maneuver our work situations, build a house on the property, and make the move. Thus began my new life on the edge of things, falling asleep to the cries of coyotes and the radiance of stars on my roof.

I came to be a teacher at Vista de las Cruces, the school near the junction of Highways 1 and 101. It is nestled by the mountains and the oaks in a place that was once a miniature community with its own inn, garage, and a little store sustained by farmers, ranchers, and travelers to the Gaviota wharf and Santa Ynez Valley. All of this had vanished by the time the school was built in the 1980s as part of a controversial settlement with the Chevron oil company, but the beautiful little school brought a new kind of vitality to the site. When I rounded the bend on my way to work each morning I could see it in a slant of sunlight, shining.

Never was the magic more apparent than the holiday season. A significant number of our students were from Mexican families who lived and worked on the surrounding ranches, and our music teacher, Victoria Ostwald, decided to tap into a tradition of that culture and organize an annual Los Posadas procession. Never mind its religious themes in a public school; it was as holy or as secular as you wanted it to be and its enchantment and good-natured sense of theater were unfailing. With Victoria at the helm, we had not just any old school band, but a string orchestra, mostly violins, whose notes unfurled in the hands of fledgling musicians in a manner less smooth than earnest, but always touching. There would be a musical performance in the auditorium, followed by the procession outdoors in the courtyard of the school.

A little Mary sat astride an actual donkey, and she and Joseph went from door to door, the classrooms as inns, each time being turned away. All the rest of us—students, teachers, neighbors, and families—followed and sang in Spanish. The strangers were refused shelter at every door, and at last they reached the manger, where the words and tempo shifted to joy and they were welcomed as holy pilgrims: *Entren, Santos Peregrinos, reciban este rincón, que aunque es pobre la morada, os la doy de corazón.*

Then the party began. We all returned to the auditorium for potluck treats and a piñata for the kids...and oh, what a happy pandemonium ensued with the walloping of the piñata! Alas, on this particular evening, someone overzealously yanked at the cord to raise the piñata higher, and it got snagged in the ceiling beams far beyond reach. A disappointed gasp rippled through the crowd, and a dapper cowboy named Billy dashed out to his pick-up truck and returned with rope in hand. He removed his hat and buckskin leather jacket, carefully eyeballed the situation, threw a perfect loop, and lassoed the piñata down from the rafters. Everyone cheered and the fun resumed. It was my fourth month living and working in Gaviota and I began to suspect that I'd stumbled into some sort of dreamland.

Now, nearly twenty years after I first came to teach here, the school bus still rattles along Rancho Real and new children wait by the mailboxes. The driver slows for deer and moseying dogs, pulling over if some kid in the back thinks he might have just seen a whale.

The place is a point of geography, a frame of mind, and a time-blurred zone where the past likes to loiter. For years the sign on Highway 101 read, "Gaviota: Population 94" and although that number may be a low-ball estimate, there are still more cattle than people. The relentless march of development has sputtered and stalled here, not unequivocally, and not enough to cease watchfulness, but enough that we can look outside and see things as they might have looked a century ago, to behold and be held by the natural word.

But being here is a work in progress, and one must quickly shed the illusion that it will ever be possible to sit back and be finished. There's always brush to clear, some window that's leaking, a phone line suddenly dead. There are mice in the car, rattlesnakes dancing right outside the door, desiccated husks of deceased sow bugs heaped beneath the couch. Water and solar power systems require constant diligence, fruit needs to be gathered before birds and bears get at it, and the infamous wind can make you crazy.

Sometimes it rains. Hopefully the pantry is stocked, and if the creek rises, it's best to be on this side of it. My neighbor Jeanne and I used to wander in the windows between rainstorms wearing tall rubber boots so we could splash around in puddles and stomp out channels in the mud to divert the water that pools in the road. There was something satisfying in seeing the currents of water rushing down the side of the dirt road through the conduits we created, and a great sense of accomplishment in observing the newly drained aftermath. Meanwhile her dog Pi would intently sniff out critters in the grass and all things dead and smelly, then bound up the hill in futile pursuit of a distant deer—or maybe in pure jubilation, which was his general frame of mind.

Once we had a diamond day. For hours the sky held out bright stretches of blue along with an ominous layer of darkness, and when raindrops finally appeared, they did not fall but hung in the air, suspended and glistening, infused with sunlight like a crystal-beaded curtain, a veritable veil of diamonds. Jeanne and I were giddy with it, fully enchanted, walking through the sparkle. You never know around here what form the magic will take. You just have to be present and lucky. Come to think of it, if you are present, you are by definition lucky.

I am writing on the day of winter solstice. The earth is at its furthest tilt from the hidden sun, and for an instant we will be suspended equidistant between the ebbing and waxing of daylight hours. The orchard is enveloped in cloud, the muddy creek is strewn with broken branches, and the sycamores have dropped broad yellow leaves. Irises whose bulbs I placed in the ground long ago have recently bloomed and swooned, their amethyst heads resting heavily on the ground.

We are always at a turning point as we spin through time and space, and this shifting world is full of mystery and wonder, more questions than answers, more yearning than resolution.

I live in a transition zone. My house is a box of light, and I am as ephemeral as air, and I shall feel what I feel, for I have lived and I have loved that much.

CPSIA information can be obtained
at www.ICGtesting.com
Printed in the USA
FSHW021450221218
54647FS